HAM CRUE 11

The Concise Dictionary of Education

Gene R. Hawes
Lynne Salop Hawes

A Hudson Group Book

 VAN NOSTRAND REINHOLD COMPANY
NEW YORK CINCINNATI TORONTO LONDON MELBOURNE

Library of Congress Catalog Card Number: 82-2605
ISBN· 0-442-26298-1

Manufactured in the United States of America

Published by Van Nostrand Reinhold Company Inc.
135 West 50th Street, New York, N.Y. 10020

Van Nostrand Reinhold Publishing
1410 Birchmount Road
Scarborough, Ontario MIP 2E7, Canada

Van Nostrand Reinhold Australia Pty. Ltd.
17 Queen Street
Mitcham, Victoria 3132, Australia

Van Nostrand Reinhold Company Limited
Molly Millars Lane
Wokingham, Berkshire, England

15 14 13 12 11 10 9 8 7 6 5 4 3 2 1

Library of Congress Cataloging in Publication Data

Hawes, Gene R.
    The concise dictionary of education.

    "A Hudson Group book."
    Includes index.
    1. Education—Dictionaries. I. Hawes, Lynne
Salop. II. Title.
LB15.H38   370′.3′21   82-2605
ISBN 0-442-26298-1   AACR2

TO
WILLIAM D. BOUTWELL
1900–1977

for many years one of the prime leaders of the very large and influential publishing operations of Scholastic Magazines, Inc., and its Scholastic Book Services;

a founder of the distinguished consulting organization in publishing management, Moseley Associates, Inc. (established as Boutwell Crane Moseley Associates, Inc., in 1971);

and enthusiast for a projected book along the lines of this one that he used to call, "Pedagese for Parents," in discussions of the idea that are still most fondly remembered.

To all who knew him, Bill was a wise, warm, gracious, and treasured friend.

Preface

Education can justly be called both the largest single industry and one of the most sensitive social barometers in the country. In the first capacity, it directly affects most Americans. In the second, it constantly generates new terms and new shades of meanings for old terms with successive shifts in our social climate.

Both capacities have been kept in view in the design of this work to serve as the most useful and convenient possible dictionary for the millions of professional educators, as well as for millions of public officials, community leaders, and parents seriously involved in education. It concentrates on meanings and terms of central importance across the entire breadth of educational practice, and throughout the entire reach of education from preschool years through postdoctoral studies and on into lifelong learning. It includes not only time-honored terms of enduring worth but current new terms such as Pell Grants, block grants, latchkey children, creationism, CEU, and preppy.

In the dictionary, words and phrases are presented in strict alphabetic order of the letters they contain regardless of word breaks. As an example, the entry for "workbook" appears before "work permit." Similarly, the entry for "standardization" precedes that for "standard score."

In addition, terms consisting of phrases are presented without inversion in order to spare readers the trouble of needless page-flipping. For example, you will find the entry for "permanent record" in the section for the letter "P," rather than in the "R" section as an entry that opens with "record, permanent." As another example, the entry for "academic year" is given in the section for "A."

Some terms of course have a number of different meanings significant in education, as in the case of "grade" and "program." For such terms with multiple meanings, we have generally given the most important or predominant sense first, and followed it with successively numbered meanings of lesser import.

In the opposite case of two or more terms that have essentially the same meaning, the term in wider use is defined while one or more synonymous terms that are less widely used appear as cross-references to the first term.

Altogether, we have done our best to make the book helpful to the many different kinds of persons who share our own depth of commitment to education. Administrators in one sector of education would need it in dealing with other sectors. Specialists such as guidance counselors, psychologists, or curriculum supervisors would consult it often for information on wide practice in other specialties. Faculty department heads and other teachers and professors would find it useful in functions like advising.

For school board members, the dictionary may often help them rapidly get their bearings in the face of strange, new educational terms. PTA officers could find it similarly productive. It should fast become well-thumbed in the offices of foundations, corporate education departments, and labor union education programs.

Students preparing for careers in teaching or other professional areas in education could draw on it to save much time and effort. Parents who are especially interested in education ought to find it fascinating and illuminating. And it should serve as a basic reference in libraries —public libraries, larger school libraries, college and university libraries, and corporate libraries among them.

These are the main kinds of readers whom we have had in mind while writing and editing the dictionary. We hope we have served them well, and of course assume full responsibility for any inadvertent lapses or errors we may have made in trying to do so.

GENE R. HAWES
LYNNE SALOP HAWES

A

A. See grading system.

A.A. See associate degree.

A.A.S. See associate degree.

AAUP. 1. American Association of University Professors, established in 1915, with offices located in Washington, DC. **2.** Association of American University Presses, organized in 1946, with offices located in New York City.

A.B. An increasingly outdated, traditional form of abbreviation for the degree of Bachelor of Arts. See bachelor's degree.

abacus. A manual calculating device consisting of a rectangular frame holding parallel rods on which are mounted beads that can be slid from one side to another. An ancient device, the abacus can be used to carry out arithmetic operations; in the U.S., it is sometimes employed as a demonstration or recreational device in the early years of schooling.

ABC. See A Better Chance.

ABC method. See phonics method.

A Better Chance (ABC). A national, nonprofit organization that provides scholarship aid and services to place minority-group students in secondary schools that have outstanding records of college preparation and college admissions placement.

ability. The quality of being able to perform a mental or physical task or action with a minimum or greater degree of success, through application of innate talent, acquired skill, acquired knowledge, or any combination of these.

ability grouping. See homogeneous grouping.

ability level. The minimum or greater degree of success with which a given mental or physical task or action can be performed; an ability level can pertain to an individual, or to the average range of ability found in a group of persons. The term is often used in education in connection with student performance on a comparative basis in a subject or study area.

abnormal. The quality of deviating from the norm, normal, or usual in persons, things, or events.

abnormal child. A child considered (or ascertained) to stand either above or well below the middle half or two thirds of the curves of normal distribution with respect to one or more measurable characteristics such as growth, physical size and capabilities, mental abilities, achievement in school subjects, and emotional stability and maturity.

absence. The state of students or teachers not being present in school or college when studies are in session, and the recording of their absence.

abstract. 1. A concise summary or recapitulation of major points in written or oral material. Specifically, the opening summary of a scholarly research report presented as a journal article or in documentary form. 2. To remove or set apart a portion or portions from a larger whole. 3. Theoretical; disembodied; not concrete; pertaining to pure form or principle rather than to representations of reality, as in "abstract painting" in art.

academe. Usually a figurative term referring to the realm of higher education in society (occasionally refers to all of education or an individual institution).

academic. 1. Referring to the institutional system of formal education within a school, college, or university. 2. Theoretical, and not of practical importance. 3. A scholarly person who works in higher education, as in, "David Reisman is a celebrated academic on the Harvard University faculty."

academic course. Traditionally, pertaining to courses that are classical, scholarly, or in the liberal arts, the substance of which is thought and ideas; for example, philosophy, history, English, as distinguished from technical studies and vocational training. Currently, often used to refer to any instructional course given within a school, college, or university.

academic credit. See credits.

academic dean. The chief academic administrator in a college or division of a university responsible to the president for the operation of the academic program, and for coordinating the work of faculty members.

academic freedom. 1. The right of teachers and students, and especially of faculty members in higher education, to express their professional views and thoughts without penalty or suppression. 2. The intellectual environment within a school or university that permits the free and unhampered flow of ideas between teachers and students, and that encourages the full exercise of intellectual abilities without restraints, restrictions, limitations, or censorship.

academic guidance. See guidance.

academic probation. See probation.

academic promotion. See promotion.

academic year. Also called the school year. The total, inclusive period of time annually, from early fall until late spring, when schools, colleges, and universities are in session with full faculty present (exclusive of summer sessions). The academic year may be divided into semesters, trimesters, quarters, or other terms, depending on the institution. See calendar.

academy. 1. A learned society whose members are scholars, such as the Academy of Arts and Sciences. 2. A private or independent school (usually on the secondary level). 3. A special school in higher education, such as a military academy.

accelerated course. A course offered for completion in less than the usual amount of time; for example, in summer session, a 14-week semester course might run for 6 weeks.

accelerated program. See acceleration.

acceleration. The process by which a student progresses through school grades or in general learning at a faster rate than the average student, and completes the required work in less time than normally allotted.

acceptance. 1. Favorable recognition of a person's worth without approving or disapproving of his or her conduct. An attitude employed frequently by teachers to improve students' self-image and motivation. 2. The granting of admission to a college or other educational institution or program.

accommodation. As used by Jean Piaget in the concept formation aspect of his theory of learning, the process by which an individual modifies current behavior in order to adjust to and meet new or additional conditions in the environment. See also Piaget, Jean.

accountability. Educational accountability is a concept in which the school system, and especially teachers, are held responsible for the learning and academic progress of students.

accounting. A subject in which students learn the functions involved and methods required by the accounting profession for keeping financial records of transactions of a business, other organization, or individual, including the summarization and explanation of these transactions.

accreditation. Approval of a professional program of studies, or of the study programs of an entire educational institution, by a recognized accrediting body; course credits and degrees are generally widely accepted if earned in an accredited program or institution. "State" accreditation represents the minimum level of such approval; it is granted by the education officials of a state (such as the state education department), and is normally provided for private (or independent) schools, noncollegiate technical institutes and other career schools (private and public), and institutions of higher education. "Regional" accreditation is granted to entire institutions by one of the six voluntary "regional associations" in the U.S. recognized for this purpose by the educational community and federal education authorities; it is granted to private and public secondary schools, noncollegiate technical institutes and other career schools (public and private), and institutions of higher education. "Professional" accreditation is granted to a program of studies in a specified professional or occupational area by a professional association recognized for this purpose by federal education authorities and by the educational community; programs are professionally accredited in a great many areas, such as architecture, business, dentistry, engineering, law, medicine, optometry, and pharmacy. Professional accreditation is granted to programs at institutions of higher education, and in some cases to programs at career schools on the postsecondary level.

acculturation. The process occurring between groups or individuals of learning and assimilating some aspects of one another's culture, or informally, by dint of coming together and interacting. Impact can vary from simple learning of traits and characteristics to complete merging of cultures.

achievement. Successful accomplishment or performance in particular subjects, areas, or courses, usually by reasons of skill, hard work, and interest. Typically summarized in various types of grades, marks, scores, or descriptive commentary.

achievement motivation. In theory, a psychological need and energetic drive that prompts an individual to strive for and work toward mastering his or her environment by the successful accomplishment of a goal or goals, accompanied by a sense of satisfaction and self-worth. Also called achievement need.

achievement need. See achievement motivation.

achievement test. A standardized test designed to measure and compare levels of knowledge and understanding in a given subject already learned.

achiever. See latent achiever, overachiever, underachiever.

acquired ability. Skill or talent that is learned by one's own effort as differentiated from that which is innate or hereditary.

acronym. An abbreviation or word constructed from the first letters of the words in a formal or official name and used as a short reference; as examples, SAT is the acronym for *S*cholastic *A*ptitude *T*est, and NOW is the acronym for *N*ational *O*rganization for *W*omen.

ACT. See American College Testing Program.

activity curriculum. A program found sometimes in lower grades planned jointly by students and teachers in which the content is based largely upon the educational priorities or interests of the students. Closely akin to curricula in progressive education.

activity unit. See unit.

adaptation. 1. The process by which an individual alters his or her current mental, physical, or emotional behavior to meet and deal with new conditions in a learning situation. 2. Instruction to enhance learning and meet individual student differences and needs by adjusting the style, subject matter, and method of teaching. Used frequently in teaching exceptional, disadvantaged, or gifted students.

addition facts. See number facts.

adjunct professor. A title for a teacher in higher education who is not a tenured faculty member but employed in a temporary capacity or on a part-time basis.

adjustment. See life adjustment course, social adjustment.

administration. The management, organization, operation, and supervision of an educational institution. Usually includes all institution functions other than teaching.

administrative policy. A plan, set of rules, or course of action issued by a board of education or other chief administrative authority stating principles, practices, and procedures of an educational institution to guide decision-making in specific matters as they arise.

admission. 1. Formal acceptance of an applicant into a course of study or school through having satisfied admissions requirements and having proven qualified in other respects. See admissions requirements, admissions test, early admission, early decision plan. **2.** The function and department of a college, university, or school concerned with applicants and with the institution's admissions policies and their application; also called admissions. See also competitive admissions, open admissions, rolling admission, selective admissions.

admissions requirements. A statement by a college, school, or program to which prospective students must apply for admission, specifying the types of information (such as transcripts of prior study, recommendations, and scores on entrance tests) that are required for admission. The requirements also often include identification of minimum kinds and amounts of preparatory study required, and in some cases include identification of minimum levels of academic qualifications required, such as the applicant's rank in class.

admissions test. Examination required of applicants for admission to an educational institution or program; uniform admissions tests developed by specialized educational organizations tend to be widely used for college and graduate admissions in higher education. Also often called entrance examination in past decades.

Admissions Testing Program (ATP). A major program of The College Board offering standardized tests widely required for college admission, including the Board's Scholastic Aptitude Test, and its Achievement Tests (in a number of individual subjects). See College Board; Scholastic Aptitude Test.

Admission Test for Graduate Study in Business (ATGSB). An examination that was widely required for admission to graduate schools of business, and that has been succeeded in recent years by the Graduate Management Admissions Test (GMAT). See Graduate Management Admissions Test.

adolescence. The chronological years of individual growth and development beginning with the onset of puberty (about 13 years old) and lasting more or less until maturity (about 21 years old). The adolescent is past childhood and not yet an adult, so that the physical and psychological processes of development may be erratic or confusing and lead to difficulty in adjustment or adolescent crisis.

adolescent crisis. See adolescence.

adolescent spurt. A sudden and obvious acceleration of some adolescent feature of growth such as height, as reflected in observations like, "He grew two inches overnight."

adult education. Education for men and women of all ages provided by schools, learning centers, or other agencies, which enables them to improve their general knowledge by either continuing their education or resuming incomplete education of previous years. Adult education is usually more flexible in structure than traditional, mandatory education. Adult education offerings include courses both for credit toward higher education degrees and for non-degree-credit learning. See continuing education, lifelong learning.

ad valorem tax. A tax proportionate to some stated value, for example, the real-estate property tax charged in proportion to assessed valuation that is the source of most local funding for public schools in the U.S.

advanced course. A course that goes beyond basic and intermediate courses in thought and content. Before being permitted to enroll in an advanced course, the student is usually required to have taken basic and intermediate courses as prerequisites.

advanced placement. The granting by a college (or other school or program in higher education) of academic status higher than that of typical beginning entrants to a student qualifying for such advanced placement by reason of prior learning, evidenced by performance on examinations, or by transcript of prior coursework and credit which the student is transferring. Advanced placement by a college may or may not include granting also of degree credit to the student receiving advanced placement. Also called advanced standing.

Advanced Placement Program (APP). A major program of The College Board offering suggested course outlines of college-level courses in each of about a dozen subjects for teaching by secondary schools. Also provides annual administration of corresponding examinations by which high school students who have taken the courses can obtain degree-credit for the courses from the colleges they later attend.

advanced standing. See advanced placement.

adviser. A qualified and informed person on staff who aids students by providing them with specific information in a given area. (Sometimes spelled "advisor.") See faculty advisor, student advisor.

advisory committee. A group of people with either similar or varied expert knowledge in certain areas, who counsel educational administrators regarding programs, problems, or issues. May or may not include personnel with the institution being advised.

aesthetics. The study of the nature of forms of beauty as represented in courses dealing with art history, the fine arts, or the philosophy of art.

A.F.A. Associate in Fine Arts degree; see associate degree.

affective domain. The realm of feelings, emotions, and attitudes in people as distinct from the cognitive domain. Students often gain support in the learning situation when their positive feelings and attitudes can be summoned as motivation.

affiliated school. An elementary or secondary school associated with a teacher-preparation college that provides the college's students with required experience in student teaching. An affiliated school is separate from the college and operates independently. Also called a cooperative school.

affirmative action. Positive action in educational institutions designed to equalize opportunity for admission of minority ethnic and racial groups of students, and to equalize opportunity for employment and promotion of women and minority-group members as faculty members and administrators.

Afro-American studies. See black studies.

AFT. See American Federation of Teachers.

age. See compulsory education, mental age, school age.

aggregate attendance. In primary and secondary schooling, the sum total of all the days on which one or more pupils are present while school is in session during the school year or portion thereof (exclusive of holidays, summers, and other days when school is closed). Aggregate attendance can be significant in grading pupils who may have been absent for long periods of time.

aggressive behavior. Conduct characterized by opposition, hostility, and attack. Students exhibiting aggressive behavior may present behavior problems that interfere with the learning process.

agricultural extension services. See extension agent.

aide. See teacher aide.

A.L.A. Associate in Liberal Arts degree; see associate degree.

alienation. A mental state of feeling separated or estranged from an individual group, or society; commonly evidenced in the behavior of adolescents during secondary school and college years as they adjust to approaching adult status.

all-year school. A school that is open and in regular session during the entire calendar year rather than during just the traditional school year from early fall to late spring.

alma mater. **1.** Latin term (cherishing or fostering mother) for the college or school attended by a former student at that institution; see also alumnae. **2.** A hymnlike song expressing special affection for the college or school.

alphabet method. See phonics method.

alternate school. Location where schooling is conducted other than the regular school site, usually due to difficulty such as fire or teacher strike.

alternative school. Usually a school or school program adapted to provide more personal attention and flexibility than conventional programs, and designed to meet the needs of students who might otherwise become drop-outs. These substitute school programs usually differ from traditional programs in curriculum, teaching methods, and background of teachers.

alumnae, alumni (plural). Former students or graduates of an educational institution (feminine singular, alumna; masculine singular, alumnus).

alumni matching grants program. See matching grants program.

A.M. An increasingly outdated, traditional form of abbreviation for the degree of Master of Arts. See master's degree.

American College Testing Program (ACT). A nonprofit educational organization based in Iowa City, Iowa, that offers the widely used battery of "ACT" tests for college admissions. Also offers other services related to college admissions, including ones for analyzing family financial need in connection with student financial aid, and the Proficiency Examination Program (PEP) for earning degree-credit by examination.

American English. The English language as used in the United States. There are substantial differences between American English and British English in spelling, meaning, idiom, and pronunciation.

American Federation of Teachers (AFT). A major labor union for teachers that is affiliated with the AFL-CIO. One of its largest constituent locals is the United Federation of Teachers (UFT) based in New York City.

American Montessori school. See Montessori method.

American Open University. An external degree college for adult learners projected for introduction in 1982 by the University of Mid-America and generally inspired by the Open University in Great Britain. See external degree programs, Open University, University of Mid-America.

analysis. A mental skill in which, when a student is confronted with a problem in his or her studies, the student breaks down the whole problem into smaller, separate components for clearer comprehension. Analysis precedes synthesis and solution.

Annapolis. The popular but unofficial name for the Unites States Naval Academy at Annapolis, MD, that is a specialized college operated by the Navy to prepare career officers.

annual. See yearbook.

annual report. In the case of some schools, school systems, and institutions of higher education, a report issued after the end of the school or academic year to inform the public about the developments, accomplishments, and problems of the year; written by the school prinicpal or head, school system superintendent, or college president.

answer grid. For purposes of grading or hand-scoring, an answer key for an objective or multiple-choice test that consists of a sheet of stiff paper in which holes are punched. The holes are located so that, when the grid sheet is aligned precisely on top of a student's completed answer sheet for the test, only the spaces for correct answers appear in the holes. The student's correct answers can thus be rapidly totaled for scoring his or her test performance.

answer key. A list of the correct answers to a set of questions on a quiz or on a test that is one of the types of short-answer tests. See also answer grid.

answer sheet. A sheet of paper on which the student is asked to mark or write the correct answers to a test; most often, a printed sheet that accompanies a printed test booklet presenting the questions of a standardized, multiple-choice test.

anthropology. The branch of the social sciences dealing with the scientific study of human beings in ways that have become distinctive to this academic discipline. Major divisions of anthropology include: archaeology, the study of the physical remains of prehistoric and extinct human cultures; ethnology, the study of human cultures through analytic and comparative methods of either archaeology or ethnography, the study of living cultures; linguistics, the study of language; and anthropometrics, the study of comparative measurements of the human body.

anti-intellectualism. Any movement or attitude opposed to the pursuit of intellectual interests, and hence usually marked by hostility to higher learning and academic freedom.

Antioch Plan. See cooperative work-study program.

antisocial. Characteristic of attitudes and behavior at odds with accepted social standards; aloof from normal, harmonious social relationships. Some adolescents may exhibit antisocial behavior as a typical part of their development.

A.O.S. See associate degree.

aphasia. A dysfunction in the sensory area affecting ability to understand words and in some cases affecting the ability to speak. Commonly believed to result from brain impairment.

APP. See Advanced Placement Program.

application fee. A fee typically amounting to $10 or more that is charged applicants who file formal applications for admission to private and public colleges and universities, and to private schools; often waived by the institution in the case of disadvantaged applicants.

applied. When preceding names of subject-matter areas such as arts, mathematics, or sciences, signifies practical studies involving the subject as opposed to purely theoretical or aesthetic studies in that subject. See applied music.

applied music. Instruction in the actual performance of music, as contrasted to instruction in harmony, counterpoint, composition, and other theoretical studies in music.

applied research. See basic research.

appreciation course. A course, offered typically in higher education and in an area of the fine arts or music, that is designed to develop general understanding and enjoyable response to the works of art treated.

apprentice. An individual, typically a young adult, who has entered a training program of apprenticeship to become a certified practitioner of a skilled trade or other occupation; among many occupations for which persons qualify as apprentices are those of electricians, plumbers, machinists, and carpenters. Apprenticeship programs involve substantial amounts of on-the-job training and are recognized in federal law and regulation.

aptitude. A capacity or talent, both innate and developed, for successful performance in one or another area, and especially for future development of capability in the area. For example, individuals may have mathematical aptitude, "verbal" aptitude with words, musical aptitude, or mechanical aptitude.

aptitude test. An examination, usually in the form of a standardized, multiple-choice test, designed to assess one or more types of aptitude.

arbitration. The process of having disputed matters placed before an impartial third party. For example, under collective bargaining agreements between professional educators such as teaching personnel, and employers such as school districts or colleges. Arbitration and its findings may be either voluntary or binding for the prime parties to the dispute.

archaeology. See anthropology.

architecture. The study of the art, science, and profession concerned with the design and construction of buildings. Historical styles and artistic and scientific aspects of design are combined in study.

archives. Often voluminous collections of authoritative records and data. Usually the subject matter is historical, but can be in music, photography, or other fields.

area studies. Fields of interdisciplinary instruction and research in higher education concerned with particular geographic regions, as in the case of Latin American Studies or Southeast Asian Studies. Area studies usually involve advanced learning drawing on such subjects as language and literature, history, economics, and political science, and may be elected by students as an undergraduate major or a graduate study concentration.

Aristotle (384–322 B.C.). Greek philosopher and teacher who studied with Plato and tutored Alexander the Great. Wrote and lectured extensively on logic, ethics, rhetoric, and metaphysics. Among his best-known works in education are *Rhetoric, Politics,* and *Poetics.* His practice of lecturing in the walks of the Lyceum in Athens gave rise to the Peripatetic School. See Peripatetic School.

arithmetic. Most often, the subject concerned with the skills of dealing with numbers for practical purposes, and including the fundamental operations of addition, subtraction, multiplication, and division; in mathematics, arithmetic or number theory is a branch of algebra.

Armed Forces education. Extremely extensive programs of education and training provided for persons on active duty in the U.S. Armed Forces; includes training in "service schools" in a great many technical specialties that are often applicable in civilian occupations. Much of this military education is offered on the college level and is recognized for college credit. See credits.

Army college. Informal term referring to advanced educational institutions open only to experienced long-service officers in the U.S. military forces and preparing them for higher responsibility; two such institutions are the United States Army War College and the United States Army Command and General Staff College.

art, arts. 1. A general term for broad fields of instruction in education, usually ones concerned with such visual arts as painting, drawing, sculpture, and architecture and sometimes including additional arts such as the dance, drama, and music. See art history, fine arts, studio art. **2.** As in arts and sciences or the liberal arts, fields of study in the humanities especially literature, philosophy, and languages; see liberal arts.

art history. One of the major branches of instruction in the arts in higher education, consisting essentially of the study of both the aesthetics and the historical contexts of major works and movements in the arts through past eras; differs from art instruction in studio art, which is the practice of such arts as painting and sculpture. See also fine arts, studio art.

articulation. 1. Coordination of course content between different levels in the educational system to promote continuing progress of students from kindergarten through higher education. **2.** The process of speaking, or a spoken utterance.

artificial intelligence. Capabilities of machines and especially of computers to perform functions like the mental processes of human beings.

arts and sciences. See liberal arts.

A.S. See associate degree.

assembly. A gathering of students, often with faculty, staff, and visitors, for purposes such as presenting general and specific programs, group learning, and making announcements. An assembly is held usually in the school auditorium.

assessment. 1. Measurement or other systematic evaluation of important elements involved in education, such as competencies or achievement in subject areas by pupils, or the relative effectiveness of teaching methods or school programs. **2.** In taxation to support public schools, the process of determining the assessed valuation of each parcel of real estate as a basis for calculating the amount of annual property tax due. **3.** Informally, either the assessed valuation or the tax amount.

assignment. A learning task, such as reading a specified textbook passage or working specified problems, given by the teacher to a student or class; an assignment must usually be completed by a time given by the teacher, and may call for the work to be done either outside class or in class.

assimilation. In the learning theory of Jean Piaget, the process by which the individual child is exposed to, absorbs, retains, and integrates new knowledge and experience into already organized and functioning systems of thought and behavior. See Piaget, Jean.

assistant. Nontenured employment position in higher education as an aide to one or more faculty members as either a "teaching assistant" or a "research assistant." Such positions or "assistantships" pay modest salaries through the academic year and are often awarded as financial aid to graduate students.

assistant professor. See professor.

assistantship. See assistant.

associate degree. The two-year college degree in the United States, awarded on completion of full-time study programs on the level of the first two years of higher education by such two-year postsecondary institutions as community colleges. Names of differing types of associate degrees parallel those of bachelor's degrees; popular types of associate degrees include: Associate in Arts (A.A.), Associate in Science (A.S.), Associate in Applied Science (A.A.S.), and Associate in Occupational Studies (A.O.S.).

associate in. See associate degree.

associate professor. See professor.

astronomy. The science concerned with outer space, with physical phenomena in the universe beyond the earth and its atmosphere.

ATGSB. See Admission Test for Graduate Study in Business.

athletic coach. See coach.

athletic conference. An intercollegiate or interscholastic league organized among member institutions to regulate and often also to schedule games or meets of their teams in one or more sports; competitions for championships or other tournament play between teams of the member institutions are commonly arranged by a conference.

athletic grant-in-aid. Grant of financial aid made usually by a college to a student in recognition of unusually high athletic ability, and often subject to many requirements by intercollegiate sports leagues and associations. Also termed athletic scholarship.

athletic program. Athletic sports activities of a school or college beyond its offerings of courses or classes in physical education; athletic programs are often ones of intramural sports (played only among students at the institution) or interscholastic or intercollegiate sports (played by teams from different institutions).

athletics. See athletic program.

athletic scholarship. A grant of student financial aid made to a student with outstanding ability in one or more intercollegiate sports; most often termed athletic grant-in-aid.

atlas. 1. A bound collection of maps often used in teaching concerned with geography. **2.** A bound collection of charts, tables, and plates used to illustrate any subject.

ATP. See Admissions Testing Program.

attendance. See aggregate attendance.

attendance law. Law enacted by any one of the states in the United States concerning attendance requirements in both public and private schools; typically, provisions include compulsory school attendance up to a specified age, and a minimum number of days required for schools to be in session.

attendance officer. An official of a public school system responsible for investigating those absences of students taken without parental consent or valid excuses; formerly referred to as truant officer, a term now obsolete.

attendance register. An official school record listing the attendance by day and class of every student enrolled in the school. It is generated from teachers' attendance reports.

attendance zone. See school attendance zone.

attention span. The length of time that an individual is able to concentrate on a particular task or learning activity. Attention span tends to be short among younger schoolchildren and typically increases as children mature.

attitude. A general predisposition or mental set with regard to any persons, beliefs, or other entities; educational systems typically seek to encourage the development of certain attitudes in their students, in addition to inculcating knowledge.

audiolingual. In study of a foreign language, methods of teaching, learning, or examination that involve listening abilities and speaking abilities in the language; also called by the obsolescent terms, oral-aural and aural-oral.

audiometer. A diagnostic device for testing the hearing thresholds of pupils, with such testing often done in primary grades by the school nurse and with referral to specialists of children whose test results indicate possible hearing problems.

audiovisual (AV) aid. A type of material that enhances learning through special appeal to hearing and sight, such as phonograph records, audio tapes, films, slides, and graphs and diagrams large enough to display before groups.

audit. In higher education, to attend class sessions in a course without the intention of securing a grade or degree-credits for the course; requires special permission, and at some institutions may be tuition-free.

auditorium. A large room or a separate building designed like a theater with rows of seats and a stage. Its purpose is to present programs of various kinds to large numbers of people. An auditorium is usually part of an educational institution.

aural-oral. See audiolingual.

austerity budget. Under the education laws in some states, the minimum budget of a public school district that is mandated by the state for a given school year after an originally larger school budget projected for the year has been rejected by the voters in the district. A number of school services and programs such as hot lunches, driver education, or remedial reading may be dropped under an austerity budget.

authoritarian. Pertaining to control by the authority in charge of a group that leaves little or no room for the exercise of freedom by other persons in the group; hence, in teaching by an individual or an institution, teaching methods that dictate thought, activity, and con- clusions to the learners and preclude independent thought or choice. Similarly, in educational administration, methods that leave teachers and other staff members little or no initiative in thought and action.

autistic child. A severely disturbed and possibly schizophrenic child requiring extensive special education; behavior includes inability to distinguish fantasy from reality and alternate acting-out and with- drawal.

autoinstruction. The teaching of oneself, usually with learning ma- terial prepared in a special form and in a formal educational program. See programmed instruction.

automatic promotion. The practice in primary and secondary school- ing of advancing pupils from one grade to the next higher grade at the end of the school year regardless of the educational attainment of the pupils. Also called social promotion, or chronological promotion.

autonomy of school district. See local autonomy.

auxiliary services. In educational institutions, the nonteaching ser- vices designed to support the academic programs, such as guidance counseling, library assisting, and lunch monitoring.

AV aid. See audiovisual aid.

average. 1. A number expressing the central tendency of a group of numbers, like the test scores of all students in a class. Unless other- wise indicated, average usually signifies the arithmetic mean (the sum of the numerals in the group divided by the number of members in the group). Other types of averages include the median (such that half the numerals in the group are larger and half are smaller than the median value), and the mode (the most frequently occurring numeral in the group). 2. In education, often refers to the average of the grades or marks in courses received by one or more students. 3. Ordi- nary or normal in some respect as against high or low in that respect. See also cumulative average, grade-point average.

B

B. See grading system.

B. Abbreviation for "Bachelor of" when used as the initial for various types of bachelor's degrees, as in B.A. and B.D. See bachelor's degree.

B.A. See bachelor's degree.

baccalaureate. Pertaining to the bachelor's degree or graduation from a four-year college.

Bachelor of Architecture (B.Arch.). See bachelor's degree.

Bachelor of Arts (B.A.). See bachelor's degree.

Bachelor of Divinity (B.D.). See bachelor's degree.

Bachelor of Laws (LL.B.). See Doctor of Jurisprudence.

Bachelor of Science (B.S.). See bachelor's degree.

bachelor's degree. 1. In all but a few cases, the four-year college degree in the United States, awarded by colleges and universities on completion of full-time study programs on the level of the first four years of higher education (which is also on graduation from a four-year college). The two most widely awarded types of such four-year bachelor's degrees are the Bachelor of Arts (B.A.) and the Bachelor of Science (B.S.); among colleges, there is no generally accepted difference in significance between these two degrees. 2. An under-graduate degree normally requiring completion of at least the first five years of higher education, such as the Bachelor of Architecture (B.Arch.) or the Bachelor of Science in Pharmacy. 3. A degree in a professional field earned by study on the graduate level, such as the Bachelor of Divinity (B.D.).

"back to basics". Recurrent slogan or trend in late twentieth-century America, urging a return to the presumably more rigorous schooling in more fundamentally important subjects or skills that had been provided in an earlier era. As an example, one widely held view of such "basics" earlier in the century was summed up in the popular reference to the "three Rs" of primary schooling: reading, writing, and arithmetic.

Bakke decision. A Supreme Court decision in 1978 upholding Allan Bakke's claim that his rights were violated by the University of California at Davis Medical School. The university, seeking through its voluntary affirmative action program to promote equal opportunity for minorities, had reserved 16 of its 100 places for minority students. Twice refused admission by the university, Bakke charged that his rejection resulted from his being denied the right to compete because of his race (white) for the 16 set-aside seats. The type of policy over-turned by the decision is referred to generally as reverse discrimination.

band. 1. Group of student musicians playing band instruments who constitute an official "school band" or "college band" representing the institution. A school or college band may be operated either as part of the music instruction program or it may be an extracurricular activity. 2. See banding.

banding. Term sometimes applied to the practice of the ability group-ing of students into a class when such practice can or does result in having students representing different grade levels assigned to the same "banded" class (for instance, a banded English class which in-cludes students with roughly the same English ability but drawn from 8th-, 9th-, and 10th-grade levels).

bar examination. An examination sponsored by each of the states that is required for admission to the bar in each state and hence for state authorization to practice law in the state; law school graduation is required for eligibility to take the bar examination, which is typically concerned with state statutes.

B.Arch. See bachelor's degree.

basal. Used primarily in elementary schooling to refer to reading textbooks or "basal readers" that are designed to present the central material in reading needed by pupils in each successive grade; applied also to other teaching materials and texts similarly viewed as central. Basal reading textbooks are also referred to as basic readers or basic reading.

basal reading. See basal.

basic course. A fundamental introductory course in a subject.

basic education. Broad term without a widely accepted special meaning, but generally understood to signify education through elementary and secondary school viewed as necessary for functioning as an independent adult, and including rigorous instruction in traditional subjects such as English and mathematics.

Basic Educational Opportunity Grant Program (BEOG). Program of grant financial aid for students in higher education that is sponsored by the federal government; since 1981, called the Pell Grant program (after Senator Claiborne Pell of Rhode Island). Grant award amounts are set annually and adjusted according to the student's demonstrated financial need; maximum amounts vary with federal funding, and ranged up to $1800 a year in the early 1980s.

basic reading. Any reading methods and materials selected to provide development in all varieties of fundamental reading skills.

basic research. In the sciences, research seeking to develop fundamental scientific theory and findings in contrast to "applied research," which is concerned mainly with developing practical applications of fundamental knowledge. Basic research is also called "pure research."

basics. See "back to basics."

basic skill. An informal term referring to fundamental skills in learning developed in elementary school, such as reading, spelling, and adding; familiarity with the term has been spread by the widely used Iowa Tests of Basic Skills, a series of elementary school achievement tests.

battered child. See child abuse.

battery of tests. A set of related standardized tests designed to be given to the same individuals at one time in order to evaluate related qualities (as with an aptitude battery that includes tests of verbal, mathematical, mechanical, and clerical aptitude, or an achievement test battery with tests in reading, English usage, arithmetic, and science).

B.D. See bachelor's degree.

behavior. The observable conduct or actions of an individual or group. Good or bad pupil behavior according to the school's rules on conduct is often marked on the student report card by teachers in elementary and secondary schools.

behavior modification. As applied in education, a method for improving classroom behavior by applying techniques which reinforce desirable actions with rewards and extinguish undesirable actions by lack of attention and rewards.

behavior norm 1. A socially defined standard for guiding proper action. **2.** The typical or average behavior in some respect; see norms.

behavior problem. Loosely used to refer to a young person who acts disruptively or abnormally, or to such behavior.

behavioral objectives. Instructional aims for a grade level, course, school, school system, or other entity stated as criteria of actual performance by students, or as descriptions of behavior that can be measured. Behavioral objectives also serve as the criteria applied in criterion-referenced testing. See criterion-referenced test.

behavioral sciences. Collective term for the fields of scientific study concerned with human behavior, including psychology, sociology, and anthropology.

behaviorism. A school of psychological thought that places prime importance on the objective study of observable behavior as opposed to ·subjective study involving introspection; developed by such psychologists as John Watson and B. F. Skinner, its theories are applied in programmed instruction, behavior modification, and other aspects of education.

bell-shaped curve. See normal distribution curve.

BEOG. See Basic Educational Opportunity Grant Program.

B.F.A. Bachelor of Fine Arts degree. See bachelor's degree.

bias. 1. Any predisposition for or against some viewpoint or social group. 2. Prejudice, or other attitude or approach, resulting in discrimination against one or more social groups, usually minority groups, and hence generally viewed as objectionable in education in a democratic nation.

Bible college. A college with an instructional program that includes the teachings of the beliefs of a Protestant Christian church denomination, usually one of an evangelical, fundamentalist nature; Bible studies are strongly emphasized at such colleges, which also often provide studies preparing teachers, ministers, and other professionals in the work of the denomination.

Bible school. A private elementary or secondary school sponsored by a Protestant Christian church denomination, usually one of an evangelical, fundamentalist nature, and strongly emphasizing Bible studies. Also called Christian school.

bibliography. A listing with essential identification of the written works pertaining to a given subject, topic, or treatment (such as an article or chapter); skills in using and compiling bibliographies are generally viewed as very important for high school students and essential for college students.

bilingual education. 1. In locales where young people are fluent in one or another of two native languages, the offering of instruction in all subjects for those young people in either native language. 2. In education in the U.S., the teaching of all subjects to non-English-speaking students in public schools in their native language while also teaching them English as a second language, until they develop sufficient English proficiency to shift to instruction in all subjects conducted in the English language. A federal law, the Bilingual Education Act of 1968, defined entitlement of students to bilingual education in this sense.

bilingualism. Fluency in two languages.

Binet, Alfred. See Binet-Simon Scale.

Binet-Simon Scale. A pioneering means for evaluating human intelligence developed in France by Alfred Binet and Theodore Simon from 1905 to 1911. See Stanford-Binet Intelligence Scale.

biology. Broadly, the science of life; often today called the biological sciences or life sciences in view of its inclusion of many sciences such as anatomy, botany, zoology, genetics, and ecology.

birth control. Voluntary regulation of the biological process of conception by various techniques of contraception for preventing unwanted pregnancies. Also broadly called family planning, birth control is taught in some schools and colleges as part of courses in such subjects as biology, health, or family life.

black colleges. Institutions of higher education that were founded in the years after emancipation of the Negro slaves in the Civil War in order to open opportunity for higher education to blacks, especially throughout the former slave-holding and border states of the U.S. Often referred to as Negro colleges in past decades, the institutions are now also frequently termed predominantly black or traditionally black colleges.

black English. A dialect of the Standard English language of the U.S. which is used by numbers of black Americans and which differs from Standard English in certain features of pronunciation, grammar, spelling, idiom, and meaning. Black English may vary in details by local or geographic subculture and other background factors.

black studies. Courses offered, usually on the level of higher education, that treat the history, literature, arts, culture, and any other aspects of the life of Afro-Americans, including their past development as black Africans. Also called Afro-American studies.

blocked time. Extended instructional period that results from the practice of combining two or more regular time periods of the school-day schedule into one longer subject or class period for the purpose of more sustained instruction.

block grant. A form of federal education aid to states that was proposed by the Reagan Administration in 1981; in it, the practice of providing grant-of-aid funds to a state in which specified sums were allocated categorically by purpose would be discontinued. Instead, the state would receive a "block grant" and allocation of various parts of the grant among various purposes would be decided by the state. Reductions in total amounts of federal aid to education were proposed at the same time.

Board of Education. Also widely termed the school board, this body consists of elected or appointed officials who carry prime responsibility for the governance and finances of the local school district or municipal school system under state education laws in the U.S. The board for a large school system rarely has more than 25 members, while the board of a typical school district often has fewer than 10 members.

boarding school. An elementary or secondary school at which substantial numbers of students reside in school dormitories during school sessions instead of at home; almost all boarding schools are private institutions which charge fees for room and board as well as tuition. Sometimes called residential school.

bonding limits. Maximum amounts set under state laws for the total indebtedness for which school districts may become liable through school-district bond issues. See bond issue.

bond issue. In education, primarily a body of uniform, interest-bearing securities in the form of bonds that are made available at one time by a public school district. A bond issue is designed to provide capital funds for a designated need like new building construction, and advance approvals required customarily include one by voters in the district. Increases in school taxes are almost always needed in order to pay the fixed interest on the bonds and to accumulate monies needed to retire the bonds (by repayment of their purchase value) when they mature after a stated period such as 20 or more years.

book learning. Conversational term for theoretical learning from books, in contrast to learning through actual practice and experience.

bookmobile. A traveling library in a motor vehicle, often used in rural areas, which visits schools and in some instances appears at school events for the purpose of encouraging students to read books.

borderline child. Informal term referring to a child viewed by school personnel as on the border between two types of conditions, such as normal or abnormal, passing or failing, and healthy or ill.

borderline intelligence. See mentally retarded.

botany. The biological science concerned with plants and plant life.

Boy Scouts. A widely popular organization for boys focused largely on outdoor activities; established in Great Britain in 1908 and now worldwide. See Girl Scouts.

Braille. A method of printing or writing that enables the blind to read through the sense of touch; it uses patterns of raised points or dots to represent letters and other characters. It is named for Louis Braille (1809–1852).

brain-damaged child. A child who has apparently suffered injury to the brain during or after birth, as evidenced by moderate to severe impairment in normal functioning in one or more of three respects: learning capabilities, motor control of physical movement, and emotional stability. The brain-damaged child usually requires special education. See special education.

brain drain. 1. Figurative term originally introduced to dramatize the massive movement of individuals with valuable intellectual qualities from their native countries to the United States. 2. Any substantial departure of talented individuals from one locale or one field of work to a second locale or field that offers greater attractions or rewards.

brainstorming. A technique used to stimulate production of creative solutions to problems by a group or individual; in it, persons are encouraged to generate spontaneously as many ideas and associations as possible without any self-consciousness or restraint. Many inapplicable ideas may be collected in the process but one or two highly valuable notions can appear among them.

brainwashing. See thought control.

bright child. 1. Among educators and in psychology generally, a child who is well above average in measured mental ability and academic achievement. 2. Informal term for a child who seems unusually impressive in mental abilities.

Broad Jump. See Prep for Prep.

"Brown vs. Board of Education of Topeka". Term referring to the landmark decision of the U.S. Supreme Court in 1954 that ended legal sanction for the segregation of blacks in the public schools, based on the name of the case before the Court. See integration.

Bruner, Jerome S. (1915–). American psychologist and educator, best known for his research studies in the cognitive growth of children and his writings in this area.

B.S. See bachelor's degree.

Buckley Amendment. See Family Educational Rights and Privacy Act.

budget hearing. Open meeting held at the time of presentation of proposed school budget for parents, school personnel, and other members of the community. A free and lively exchange of views, ideas, complaints, and suggestions usually takes place at a budget hearing. See also austerity budget, school budget.

bull session. Colloquial term for an intimate, informal discussion among a small group of students in which personal, social, and general problems and ideas are discussed in confidence. Common among adolescents and young adults, and helpful because of peer feedback.

bullying. Aggressive physical or verbal behavior by a person who seeks to intimidate or coerce another person into assuming a subservient role.

bureaucracy. An elaborate hierarchical administrative organization, at times associated with inefficiency because of diffuse authority and rigidity; the organizations administering large educational systems are in some cases called bureaucracies.

bursar. A college administrative officer responsible for handling finances, and often the one in charge of collecting payments of student fees.

business administration. In higher education, the broad field of instruction and study concerned with the management of organizations and especially business corporations; among specialties it includes are accounting, marketing, banking, finance, and investment, and human resources or personnel management. Also called management, especially when viewed as including public administration (management in government or nonprofit organizations) as well as business administration.

business education. 1. Very broad and diverse field of instruction developing capabilities for work in business or financial administration. In higher education, business education is provided primarily through very widespread two-year M.B.A. programs offered by graduate schools of business at universities, and in bachelor's programs in business administration offered by four-year colleges. Extensive programs in business education are also offered by two-year community colleges and private junior colleges, public and private technical institutes and trade schools, vocational high school programs, and corporate employee training programs. 2. A branch of professional teacher education concerned with the preparation of teachers of secretarial studies and other business subjects in secondary and post-secondary schools.

business manager. Title of an administrative officer with a school, school system, college, or university who is responsible for the institution's business affairs.

business school. 1. Informal term used to refer to a university's graduate school of business administration or to an undergraduate college of business administration. 2. A postsecondary school offering career training in business fields; see secretarial school.

busing. 1. The transporting of young people to school by school buses. 2. Reassignment and transportation of young people to public schools other than those of their neighborhoods in order to achieve school desegregation by correcting racial imbalance, done at times when a court issues orders to a school district under legal requirements for desegregation. See integration.

busywork. Colloquial term for activity assigned to an individual or group by someone in authority mainly in order to keep the individual or group occupied; in schooling, the term is applied to such activity assigned to a class by a teacher so that the teacher may attend to other tasks.

buzz session. Colloquial term for an informal gathering to discuss certain topics or questions.

C

C. See grading system.

calendar. 1. For an elementary or secondary school, a calendar showing the days that school is in session, school holidays, school events, and all general scheduling pertinent to the school year. 2. For a college or university, a calendar showing all important dates in a given academic year.

call the roll. The act of recording attendances and absences by the teacher at a session of a class or course; also termed, take the roll.

Campfire Girls. A popular organization for girls with activities focused substantially on outdoor activities. See Girl Scouts.

campus. The physical grounds and buildings of a college or university (or of a school), setting it off as distinct and separate from other community buildings and grounds. Campus buildings include classrooms, laboratories, administrative offices, and dormitories.

candidate. 1. In frequent official usage in education, an applicant or registrant, such as a "candidate for admission" (an applicant for admission to a college, school, or program); a "degree candidate" (a student matriculated for an academic degree); and a "test candidate" (a registrant for a standardized test for admission or other purposes). 2. Any individual recognized as a contender for a particular status or office, such as a candidate for election as student body president.

Candidates Reply Date Agreement. A college subscribing to this agreement will not require any applicant offered admission as a freshman to notify it of his or her decision to attend (or to accept an offer of financial aid) before May 1. The purpose of this agreement is to give applicants time to hear from all the colleges they have applied to before they have to make a commitment to any one of them; the agreement is sponsored by The College Board.

capability. The full potential and limits of one's mental, physical, moral, or emotional developmental abilities and skills. Measured and evaluated from early schooling by teachers and by standardized testing.

cap and gown. See mortarboard.

card catalog. A reference file of cards in the school library listing all of its books and periodicals. Titles, authors, names, and sometimes subjects are indexed and cross-indexed alphabetically.

career counseling. A service function provided students, usually in a high school or college, in which information is given to a student by a counselor having current knowledge of particular career fields plus knowledge of the student's intellectual and personal abilities. Various academic records and testing measures may be used to aid in the student's career exploration and decision-making process. The function is generally termed vocational guidance when provided in a high school by a guidance counselor. See guidance.

career day. A day-long program for students sponsored by one or more colleges or high schools at which professional, business, and community representatives speak and advise on entering their respective occupations.

career education. Instructional programs in all curriculum areas in which emphasis is given to career information, guidance, and preparation for pupils. Federal education officers in the late 1960s and 1970s led efforts to encourage public schools especially to develop increased career education.

career placement. See placement.

career services. See placement.

Carnegie Commission on Higher Education. See Kerr, Clark.

Carnegie unit. A standard introduced to systematize definition of college-preparatory studies in secondary education in which one unit of secondary instruction consists of 120 hours of classroom or laboratory work in a given subject (one hour per weekday through one school year), and which provides for at least 16 units of work in a four-year secondary curriculum; originated through the Carnegie Foundation for the Advancement of Teaching. See also unit.

case history. In primary or secondary education, confidential file notes made by a guidance counselor or school psychologist containing personal records and documented study of a student's behavior and development. Students on whom case histories are kept generally present problems.

CE. Civil engineering, the branch of engineering concerned with large structures such as bridges, roads, dams, docks, and buildings.

CEEB. Acronym for College Entrance Examination Board; see College Board, The.

censorship. In education, the removal or banning of any material considered improper for possible study by students at the decision of authorities other than the professional educators at the institution in which such removal occurs. Censorship in this sense is widely viewed as a violation of academic freedom and democratic principles.

centralized administration. An administrative system in a school district in which an authoritative body is vested with the power of decision-making, jurisdiction, and control over all subunits in the district.

central school; centralized school; central school district. See consolidated school; consolidated school district.

central tendency. With respect to data such as the course grades or test scores of students in a class, the central point around which the values tend to be evenly distributed; expressed by a "measure of central tendency" such as an average.

certificate. 1. An official document of a governing body or private organization attesting to the truth of stated facts, such as the meeting of given requirements by an individual. 2. In education, a document other than a diploma or a degree that is widely awarded by post-secondary institutions to attest to the individual's completion of a specified program of study. 3. For educators, a document that attests to the meeting of state requirements by an individual for professional status or licensing in one of the professional specialties in public education, such as teaching, school psychology, guidance counseling, or school administration. See also certification.

Certificate of Advanced Graduate Studies. A type of higher education diploma issued to persons completing programs of specialized study on the graduate level, often beyond the master's degree; among such programs are ones in educational specialties like curriculum supervision, guidance, and administration.

certification. For educators, the status of full professional qualification or licensure in a professional specialty like teaching as specified in certification requirements of the state that pertain to positions in the public schools. Teacher certification or licensing may be obtained on a provisional or temporary basis and then on a permanent basis in a number of states.

CETA. See Comprehensive Education and Training Act.

CEU. See Continuing Education Unit.

chair. 1. In general, to lead in conducting a meeting or the work of a committee or similar group as its presiding officer. 2. In higher education, a position of unusually high eminence to which a professor is appointed; such a faculty chair may also be accompanied by a naming of the professorship (as in the title, "John Doe Professor of

History") and by an endowment permitting an annual salary higher than the institution's regular scale for professors.

chairperson. In secondary and higher education, a faculty member in a department who is elected by other members, or appointed by the institution's administration to serve as the leading officer of the department for a specified term. The chairperson normally represents and speaks for the department, carries its administrative responsibilities, and receives added financial compensation.

chancellor. In higher education, the title for full-time administrative office ranking above the office of president; frequently used for the chief officer of a university system consisting of institutions at individual campuses that are each headed by their own president.

checking. The act of going back over and reviewing work already done in order to ascertain its correctness, either by using the same mental processes again, or by using other confirming devices.

cheerleader. Secondary school or college student who joins with others on the cheerleading squad to perform gymnastics and conduct cheering for an athletic team of the institution when it is playing against another team. Cheerleaders help to boost morale of players and audience, wear costumes, and may be accompanied in cheering by a band.

ChemE. Chemical engineering, the engineering specialty that deals with applications of the science of chemistry.

chemistry. The science of the composition, structure, properties, and actions of systems of matter.

child abuse. An action of physical, psychological, or sexual injury to a child, done by an emotionally disturbed parent or other adult, directing aggressive behavior at the child; a victim of such abuse may be referred to in professional analysis as a "battered child." Seriously depriving a child with respect to basic life needs such as food, shelter or medical treatment represents a special type of child abuse termed child neglect.

child-care center. See day-care center.

child-centered education. An educational theory or system that emphasizes the pupil and his or her individual characteristics as central in conducting instruction instead of focusing on subject matter, external authority, and educational requirements. Curriculum is constructed according to the pupil's interests and needs. See also open education, progressive education.

child cruelty. See child abuse.

child development. The study of the intellectual, physical, psychological, and social development of the child from birth to adolescence. A required subject for study in professional teacher education programs.

child-labor laws. Federal and state statutes governing the conditions under which children may be employed outside their home, and the age at which they may be employed.

child neglect. See child abuse.

child prodigy. A child who is extraordinarily talented or advanced, usually in music or another artistic field.

Chomsky, Noam (1928–). Twentieth-century American scholar of language and linguistics, best known for his work in the field of syntax and the relationship between language and mind.

chorus. 1. A relatively large student vocal group formed for purposes of musical training and enjoyment. 2. The major section of a traditional or popular song that is repeated at regular intervals.

Christian school. See Bible school.

chronicles. Traditional term for past historical records and accounts.

chronological age. Term introduced in educational measurement to identify a child's age as ordinarily understood (but usually given in years and months) as distinct from "mental age" as evaluated by an intelligence test. See Intelligence Quotient.

chronological promotion. See automatic promotion.

church school. 1. A private school operated by a religious body or church, commonly providing comprehensive and religion-oriented schooling on the elementary and/or secondary levels plus religious teachings. **2.** Part-time religious instruction offered (often on days of worship) by a religious congregation or church for young people; also called Sunday school in a number of Christian denominations. **3.** See also Bible school, parochial school.

circuit teacher. 1. A teacher who travels between two or more schools to teach an elective or optional subject, such as art or music; also called an itinerant teacher. **2.** A teacher of handicapped students who travels to their homes or schools in order to teach them.

city-wide school. In some larger cities, a specialized public school, usually on the high school level, attended by students citywide who qualify for entrance through competitive admissions, in contrast to a public school open only to students residing in that school's attendance zone.

civics. In secondary school, a course in political science or government pertaining to citizenship.

Civil Rights Act of 1964. A federal law passed during Lyndon Johnson's administration making federal funding of public schools dependent on desegregation.

class. 1. In secondary and higher education, all students enrolled in the same course scheduled to meet in regular sessions with the same teacher during a school term, such as a history class. **2.** In elementary education, the group of pupils taught for all or most of the school day through the term by the specified teacher for that class. **3.** All students on the same grade level, such as the seventh-grade class or senior class. **4.** A group of students graduating from school or college at the same time, such as the "class" of 1970. **5.** Informal term for a session of a course, as in, "I have no French class this week." **6.** In general, social groups such as the "lower, middle, and upper classes."

class hours. Scheduled periods of instruction or laboratory work for a student.

class mother. In elementary schools, a mother of one student in a class who serves as a helper to the teacher and class by arranging class social programs and trips, and generally assisting with noninstructional activities.

class period. The uniform length of time scheduled for one session or instructional period in a course, commonly 40 minutes or 50 minutes; approximately 10 minutes are scheduled between periods to give students time to get to their next course session.

class rank. The relative numerical scholastic standing of a student in his or her class, usually calculated for a graduating class to meet admissions requirements. See grade-point average.

class size. Term often used in reference to school budget. See student-teacher ratio.

classical studies. Teaching or scholarly research in Latin and Ancient Greek languages, or in the literature of Ancient Greece and Rome.

classics. 1. Masterpieces created in past eras; works of enduring excellence in literature, art, music, and human thought in general. **2.** Originally, such works created in Ancient Greece and Rome.

classification. The result of the systematic grouping and organization of people, objects, ideas, and situations into categories based upon certain common specific traits, principles, or elements for purposes of identification and learning.

classroom climate. The atmosphere and general environment in the classroom that may help or hinder the learning process. Includes physical and material resources, emotional tone and attitude of teacher, social attitudes of peers, and rules and regulations.

classroom without walls. Term applied in the 1960s to experimental approaches in elementary school design in which instructional areas were not divided into walled classrooms of conventional size but in which the areas occupied by each of several classes were divided by partitions such as bookshelves.

clearinghouse. In education, an agency that collects and disseminates voluminous data. ERIC (Educational Resources Information Center) is a clearinghouse.

CLEP. See College-Level Examination Program.

clerical subjects. Business subjects such as typing, filing, bookkeeping, and business English.

client. The person seeking the advice of a school psychologist or a counselor at a school or college. Sometimes called counselee.

clinic. An organization or professional center, staffed by trained workers, that provides counseling, diagnosis, treatment, and follow-up at low cost in such areas as medicine, dentistry, psychiatry, and psychology. A school will frequently refer a student to a clinic.

clinical professor. A professor appointed to teach courses concerned directly with the practice of a profession, as in medicine or dentistry.

club. Student organization associated with a school or college through which members further a common interest or purpose outside of class hours; the school or college may or may not recognize a student club as one of the institution's official extracurricular activities.

cluster college. A group of colleges in close physical proximity that coordinate their operations and share services and facilities for greater effectiveness and economy; a well-known example is the Colleges of the Claremont in California.

coach. A school or college teacher proficient in physical education whom the institution appoints to the position of coach for its inter-scholastic or intercollegiate teams in one or more sports; the coach directs and trains the teams for which he or she is responsible.

coaching. 1. Providing extra instructional help to a student by tutor-ing. 2. Provision of criticism, suggestions, and evaluation to teachers by a supervisor, who has observed their classroom methods and per-formance. 3. The work or field of directing sports teams.

code. 1. A collection of rules or laws regulating behavior. 2. A col-lection of statements of principles, as in honor code. 3. A set of symbols used to represent letters, words, or numbers in communica-tion, such as Morse code or espionage code.

coed. 1. Short colloquial term for coeducational. 2. Now obsolete, a woman college student.

coeducational. Pertains to the basic feature of a school or college providing for attendance by both male and female students; institu-tions for only female students or only male students are not coedu-cational.

cognitive abilities. Mental or intellectual abilities involved in percep-tion, knowing, and abstract thinking.

collective bargaining. In education, the process analogous or identical to labor-management negotiations for new labor union contracts in which a teachers' organization negotiates with the administration of a school district or college on terms of a new employment contract for the teachers. In almost all cases, the organizations that conduct collective bargaining are school-district chapters of the National Education Association, or locals of the American Federation of Teachers.

college. 1. An institution of higher education that offers study pro-grams leading to bachelor's degrees, or shorter programs leading to associate degrees; many colleges are organized as separate institutions, while others are constituent schools of universities. 2. A graduate school of a complex institution like a university. 3. In conversational usage, any institution of postsecondary education. 4. In many nations other than the United States, an institution of secondary education. 5. A professional society or medical specialty association, such as the American College of Surgeons.

College Board, The. A national, nonprofit association with a membership of more than 2500 colleges and universities, secondary schools, and other educational associations and agencies; it provides entrance tests and other services related to admission to higher education. It is based in New York City, and its formal name is College Entrance Examination Board (CEEB).

"College Boards". Colloquial term referring usually to the admissions tests sponsored by The College Board; may also refer to any college entrance tests. See Admissions Testing Program; College Board, The.

college bulletin. See college catalog.

college catalog. A booklet or book issued by a college or university to present information needed by potential applicants and by enrolled students on such matters as course offerings, admissions requirements, financial aid, academic year calendar, and student regulations. Usually issued annually; in some cases called the college bulletin. A shortened, attractively illustrated version especially for applicants is often called the college viewbook.

college credit. See credits.

college day. A day-long program for students sponsored by one or more secondary schools at which admissions representatives of colleges give students information and guidance about their colleges. Similar programs are also offered under such names as college night or college fair.

College Extrance Examination Board (CEEB). See College Board, The.

college fair. See college day.

college guidance. See guidance.

College-Level Examination Program (CLEP). Program of The College Board providing more than 40 examinations in a range of college subjects and the frequent offering of the examinations at test centers throughout the United States and abroad; many colleges award course credits toward degrees on the basis of the examinations, enabling adult learners especially to earn course credits through self-study or experience and not only by course attendance. See College Board, The.

college night. See college day.

college of education. See teachers college.

college placement. See placement.

College Scholarship Service (CSS). A service of The College Board that assists higher education institutions, the federal government, state scholarship programs, and other organizations in the equitable distribution of student financial aid funds. By collecting confidential data on a family's financial circumstances and analyzing its ability to contribute to college costs, CSS need-analysis services offer a standardized method of estimating a student's financial need. See also Financial Aid Form.

college viewbook. See college catalog.

colloquium. An academic seminar, meeting, or course at the level of advanced study or professional scholarship.

colloquy. A formal spoken or written dialogue among educational specialists, the purpose of which is to present inquiry, encourage discussion, and resolve problems in specific educational matters.

commencement. See graduation exercises.

commerce. In higher education, a term used in previous decades to refer to study programs concerned with business and business management; such programs are commonly characterized today as ones in business administration or management. See business administration.

commercial art. In postsecondary education especially, the field of instruction preparing persons for employment as artists creating illustrations and designs used for commercial purposes in such areas as advertising and magazine and book publishing; differs from fine art or the fine arts.

commercial education. See business education.

commissioner of education. Title of the chief education officer in the state governments of a number of states in the United States.

community college. Term very widely used in the names of public junior colleges throughout the United States; a community college is one sponsored by a state, county, or other local government body that offers study programs leading to associate degrees; such a college also commonly provides wide varieties of other postsecondary study programs in occupational, technical, and cultural areas to serve community needs.

comparative education. The study of the educational systems of different countries and cultures.

compensatory education. Special educational programs that attempt to remedy deficiencies in some students' education due to socio-economic, cultural, or minority-group disadvantage, by focusing the curriculum on the needs of these students and their abilities.

competence. The state of having and demonstrating skills, abilities, or aptitudes in the satisfactory execution of a learning task.

competency-based curriculum. Type of experimental curriculum introduced in the degree programs of some colleges in the 1970s; in such curricula, degree requirements are defined not according to the customary credits earned through taking courses but by demonstration of sufficient development of sets of competencies or capabilities that are defined in detail by the college. Students are free to develop the required competencies in any way and on any schedule they choose.

competency-based education. 1. System used in elementary and secondary schooling that features the detailed definition, teaching, and demonstration by students of those competencies (involving knowledge, skills, and behaviors) that have been defined as being of central importance. Also called performance-based education. 2. Any similar instructional system in employee training, education for a profession, continuing education, or other area.

competency test. 1. Test of capabilities or skills in performing certain functions, especially such basic capabilities developed in school as reading at given levels, working practical applications of mathematics, and writing in correct English. 2. Test of this kind on which at least a passing mark is required by a state or school district for promotion of a student to the next higher grade or for receipt of the high school diploma.

competition. 1. Rivalry or vying between individuals for supremacy in working for goals such as grades, prizes, or admissions. 2. A contest to select the highest ranking contenders in some specified skill or talent.

competitive admissions. A type of admissions policy of a college or school in which the minimum qualifications that assure admission are set competitively by applicants rather than by prior definition made by the college or school; under a competitive admissions policy, the best-qualified students among those applying are admitted until all places in the entering class are filled.

composite rank. The relative standing of an individual with respect to a single value that combines indices of performance or other characteristics. See rank.

composite score. A score on an overall test made up of subtests that summarizes the separate scores on the subtests with one overall score; for example, the student's scores on the ACT college admissions test are reported as separate subtest scores in English usage, mathematics, social studies reading, and natural sciences reading, plus a summary composite score.

composition. 1. An essay or paper written by a student as assigned by a teacher in studying English or another subject. 2. A course or topic of study providing instruction and practice in the writing of such papers; also called English composition. 3. A creative product in music or the fine arts. 4. The structure, organization, or arrangement of any work.

comprehension. The mental ability to understand and grasp substantive meaning in language, thought, communication, and action. Developed through learning.

Comprehensive Education and Training Act. A federal law enacted in 1973, which provided an up-to-date charter for the manpower programs previously operated under the authority of the Manpower Development and Training Act, the Economic Opportunity Act, and the Emergency Employment Act. Grants were made available to more than 500 local and state agencies, planning and operating programs to meet local needs. See Economic Opportunity Act of 1964, Emergency Employment Act, Manpower Development and Training Act.

comprehensive examination. A test that is unusually broad in scope and far-ranging in content in an area of study. Given either at the beginning of a program of study to determine the student's preparatory levels of learning, or at the end of a program of study. For example, some colleges require a senior comprehensive examination in the student's major for graduation.

compressed speech. Recorded spoken material that is processed so that its speed is multiplied while it remains understandable; as a result, listening to a lecture or address processed into compressed speech takes only a fraction of the time occupied by its original delivery.

compulsory education. The legal requirements in all states mandating minimal school attendance annually for children between latest school-starting ages and earliest school-leaving ages specified by the individual state; states correspondingly require provision of public education through which legal school attendance requirements may be met.

compulsory school age. See compulsory education.

computer-assisted instruction. Instruction in which a computer is used to present substantial amounts of learning material to the student; it often represents an autoinstructional technique enabling students to progress at their own individual rates.

Conant report. Obsolescent informal term referring to one of two widely influential reports on education made in the 1960s by James Bryant Conant, president emeritus of Harvard University and public official: *The Education of American Teachers* (1963), and *The Comprehensive High School* (1967).

conative. In educational psychology, refers to that aspect of the individual's mental life concerned with striving through such forces as desire and volition or the will, in contrast to the aspects concerned with cognitive (intellectual) and affective (emotional) qualities.

concentration. 1. The act of directing attention toward, and becoming absorbed in, any task regardless of interruptions, and to continue doing so for a length of time. Concentration lasts longer and becomes more intense with maturation and learning. **2.** The focusing of a program or course of study in a particular subject area. In higher education, majors are areas of concentration.

concept. A valid understanding or idea of the essential nature of some entity, such as a series of events, a type of phenomenon, or a body of thought; concepts formed by a student or child may concern simple or complex entities.

concept formation. In the thought of psychologist Jean Piaget, an important aspect of the cognitive development of the child. See Piaget, Jean.

concordance. In scholarly research, an alphabetic index of the major words in a book (such as the Bible) or an author's works with references to the passages in which each word appears (and possibly quotation from and commentary on each passage).

concrete. In educational or intellectual matters, a specific, real, tangible, or perceptible thing or situation, as opposed to an imagined or abstract entity.

conditioned reflex. A new response brought about by exposure to a conditioned stimulus; also called conditioned response. See conditioning.

conditioned response. See conditioned reflex.

conditioned stimulus. A learned stimulus that is administered to replace an unconditioned or natural stimulus, and that eventually elicits the same response as the unconditioned stimulus. See conditioning.

conditioning. 1. A process in which behavior may be changed by substituting a conditioned or learned stimulus for a natural stimulus in order to elicit a conditioned or learned response. In the famous original example, Pavlov's dogs were first exposed to a bell ringing whenever they were given food and were thus conditioned to salivate by the bell-ringing even when not given food with it. 2. Special exercise or training for physical fitness or athletic competition.

conduct. 1. Behavior. 2. In education, the moral or ethical aspect of behavior. Especially important in the early elementary-school years, when pupils learn much of their socialization.

conference. 1. A meeting of two or more people for discussion on varied matters; schools regularly hold conferences between teacher and student, teacher and parent, principal and teachers, and principal and students. 2. See athletic conference.

conflict. In an individual, a clash or contention between two or more drives or desires at a given time, resulting in some mental discord; such psychological conflict may interfere with a student's learning until resolved.

conformity. A behavioral trait evidenced by an individual or group's conscious or unconscious compliance with conventional customs and social attitudes.

congenital factors. Physical or psychological influences on the prenatal growth and development of a child before birth; such factors may contribute to learning difficulties or disabilities for the child.

conscience. A faculty developed at home and in school from early childhood, functioning as the center of awareness for an individual's moral and ethical beliefs; similar in some respects to what Freudian psychoanalytic theory terms the superego.

consensus. General agreement or accord among a group of people on certain matters; consensus among professionals is frequently sought in schools for decision-making purposes.

conservatory. 1. Educational institution that specializes in teaching music, and provides instruction in many areas of music to prepare students for musical careers. 2. An institution offering broad instructional programs both in music and in theatrical arts.

consolidated school; consolidated school district. A consolidated school is a public school formed by the merger of two or more smaller public schools with the intention of offering better and broader coursework and other educational services; also called central or centralized school. A consolidated school district is one similarly formed by merger of two or more smaller districts, and may similarly be called a central school district.

consortium. A special joint endeavor of a group of institutions of higher education which cooperatively operate a project for designated educational or research purposes.

consultative services. Guidance counseling services that draw on the help of consultants of various kinds, such as psychiatrists, physicians, nurses, social workers, and professionals in a number of career areas who can provide information on those areas.

content-centered education. An educational system in which major emphasis is placed on subject-matter content (rather than on the learning-process or on the child); content-centered approaches tend to feature traditional teaching methods. See child-centered education, process-centered education.

context. 1. The larger and extended portion of written material or spoken statement in which a word, phrase, or sentence is used, with the larger portion giving meaning to the word, phrase, or sentence. **2.** The surrounding circumstances in which an event occurs, bearing a relationship to the event.

continuing education. Further education offered primarily for adults of all ages on postsecondary levels; includes extensive programs designed to keep such professionals as attorneys, physicians, and engineers up-to-date in their fields. Also includes many varieties of degree programs designed especially for adults, career-counseling, and career-change services, and programs of noncredit courses. See lifelong learning.

Continuing Education Unit (CEU). A unit widely used in American higher education and in noncollegiate education for adults, such as corporate education programs for employees, to quantify the amount of noncredit coursework that an individual has completed. In the cooperatively developed official definition, one continuing education unit is ten contact hours of participation in an organized continuing education experience under responsible sponsorship, capable direction, and qualified instruction.

continuous school census. An official record kept of pupil population, in which the number of children (usually until age 21) living within a school district is checked and verified periodically. Recorded in addition to the child's name is the date of birth, address, names of parents, and family size.

contraception. See birth control.

contract learning. Instructional system providing for independent study used by some nontraditional colleges and secondary schools; in it, the student enters into a "contract" or written agreement with the teacher specifying the learning tasks the student will carry out for the next long segment of a course. On completion, the student's contracted work is graded by the teacher and a new contract is mutually adopted. One of the system's originators was the Dalton, Massachusetts school system, and in past years the approach was at times called the Dalton Plan. Also called performance contract learning.

controlled experiment. A scientific experiment in which attempts are made to avoid having the results influenced by any factors other than those being investigated, with factors not being investigated said to be "controlled." One widely used technique for controlling factors in experiments in medicine and education consists in the use of "matched" groups of persons; in this approach, one group serves as the "experimental" group while the other serves as the "control" group.

controlled reading. The regulation (usually in a reading laboratory) of a reader's speed and choice of reading material by a teacher, and the use of special devices and techniques to check the reader's rate and comprehension.

convention. 1. A regional or national meeting of an association such as a political party or professional society, as in the case of a National Education Association convention. 2. A widely used practice in a culture or field of human activity that has become a custom. 3. A written agreement or pact, usually between nations.

convent school. A private school operated by a Roman Catholic convent. Curriculum is oriented around the tenets of Catholicism and includes religious instruction.

convergent thinking. Mental activity that tends to answer questions and analyze problems by using intellectual approaches that are conventional, safe, and prescribed, and that look for only one right answer; viewed as an uncreative mode of thinking. See divergent thinking.

conversion of scores. The process of translating test scores from one form of measurement to another for purposes of more meaningful comparison, as in changing standard-scale scores on a test to percentile-rank scores.

cooperating employer. An employer who hires a student from a college or vocational school for part-time employment under the auspices of a cooperative work-study program. See cooperative work-study program.

cooperating teacher. A secondary or elementary school teacher who provides a student-teacher with classroom supervision, guidance, and assistance for one term as part of the student-teacher's requirement of supervised teaching experience for a license to teach. Also called supervising teacher.

cooperation. Working together harmoniously with another person or with a group; cooperation between the child and others is stressed in school from early grades onward.

cooperative house. A type of student residence affiliated with some colleges that functions as a form of financial aid by enabling students living at the house to obtain low-cost room and board through cooperative operation of the house; in such operation, each resident contributes scheduled work in areas like cooking, cleaning, and maintenance.

cooperative nursery school. A nursery school that draws on contributed auxiliary parent services for teachers and children, with each parent giving a few hours at a time for such activities as distributing materials, dressing and undressing children, and supervising class trips. Tuition fees are usually lower in cooperative nursery schools than in noncooperative nursery schools.

cooperative work experience program. See cooperative work-study program.

cooperative work-study program. Special program offered by a college and university in which students alternate work and study, usually spending a number of weeks in full-time study and a number in full-time employment away from the campus. At times referred to as the Antioch Plan because Antioch College was one of the earliest institutions to introduce such a program.

coordinator. 1. In some large public school systems, title for a supervisory position for a teacher not in the classroom who coordinates the work of a number of classroom teachers. 2. Title variously applied to other positions in education involved with coordination.

coping. The act of dealing with difficulties and stressful situations with some degree of equanimity, and without altering one's goals. An important element in the student's emotional development and in maturation.

core course. A required, beginning subject course which is considered fundamental to the educational development of the student, such as an introductory course in English, math, history, or science.

core curriculum. A school curriculum with common requirements for all students in basic courses in fields such as English, mathematics, history, or science.

corporal punishment. Physical beating or spanking of a student for punishment; today, a generally outmoded technique of punishment in school.

corporate education. See employee education.

correctional education. Programs of classes and workshops conducted for inmates in prisons (when funds are available), with emphasis on teaching vocational and recreational skills.

correlation coefficient. In statistics, a number between zero and 1.00 that is used to indicate the degree of relationship between two sets of measurements for a representative group of individuals, such as their scores on a test and their average freshman-year grades; theoretically perfect correlation is indicated by 1.00, and actually calculated correlations are decimal numbers such as 0.37 or 0.62.

correspondence course. A type of course conducted by written instruction with teacher and student interacting by mail; in such a course, the teacher periodically sends written assignments to the student according to the course syllabus and the student completes and returns the required work. The taking of correspondence courses is called home study. Some colleges provide extensive offerings of college-credit correspondence courses. Other institutions offering correspondence courses predominantly in occupational areas are called correspondence schools.

correspondence school. See correspondence course.

counseling. See career counseling, guidance.

counterculture. 1. Broadly, the style of living and cultural attitudes espoused by the dissident "hippie" youth movement of the 1960s and 1970s, chiefly in the United States. 2. By analogy, any alternate form of cultural life proposed in opposition to the conventional culture in a society.

county school. A primary or secondary school administered by a board of education having county-wide authority. In small counties, students from the entire county may be enrolled in a county school.

course. 1. A unit of instruction in a particular subject, such as "Introductory Chemistry" or "Twentieth Century French Literature." Instruction in the form of courses is offered predominantly in secondary and higher education. Courses consist of regularly scheduled class sessions of one to five (or more) hours per week throughout the term. A diploma program or degree program is made up of a specified number of designated types of required and elective courses. See credits. 2. Loosely, as in "a course of study," a program of studies consisting of a number of individual courses.

cramming. A method of preparing to take an examination by employing a last-minute, hurried type of review in lieu of a well-organized review scheduled to provide sufficient time.

crash course. A course or program of study designed to provide education or training in a subject area in much less time than normally required.

creationism. A theory put forward by persons of fundamentalist, evangelical Christian belief to account for the creation of human beings and other forms of life in the ways reported in the Bible; also called scientific creationism and supported by arguments designed to be scientific. Pressure has been brought to bear by fundamentalist groups and state legislators to have creationism taught along with or instead of the Darwinian Theory of evolution in science instruction in public schools.

creativity. In popular understanding, originality, expressiveness, and imaginativeness, in finding new answers to problems and doing unusually good work in the arts. High creativity may or may not accompany above-average intelligence. Some highly creative students may be referred to as "gifted."

credentials. Written documents that certify an individual's qualifications in such respects as experience, education, or character, submitted usually when applying for admission, employment, promotion, or professional status.

credit by examination. A practice by colleges in which they apply policies adopted by the individual college for granting degree credits to students who earn credit-qualifying scores on tests recognized for awarding credit by the college; tests widely recognized for credit include the Advanced Placement Examinations, College-Level Examination Program (CLEP) tests, and Proficiency Examination Program (PEP) tests.

credit course. A college course that carries academic credit toward a degree. See credits.

credit-no credit. A form of pass-fail grading system; see grading system.

credits. Units that are used by institutions of higher education to record the successful completion of courses of instruction (or equivalent amounts of learning accomplished in other ways). Each credit usually indicates the number of hours per week the student is expected to attend the course over the entire term. The catalog or bulletin of the college or university defines the number and type of credit required to earn each type of degree it offers, and states the value in terms of degree credit – or "credit hours" or "credit points" – for each course offered. Also termed degree credits or credit, course credit, academic credit, or college credit. See advanced placement, credit by examination, life-experience credit, tax credit.

Cremin, Lawrence A. (1925-). Professor of education and president at Teachers College, Columbia University. An historian and interpreter of education, his writings include *The Transformation of the School* (1961), *Traditions of American Education* (1977), and *Public Education* (1976).

criminal justice. See law enforcement.

criminology. The study of crime and of criminals in their social context, usually considered to be a branch of sociology.

criteria. Established guidelines for standards, norms, or levels against which any entity may be compared or evaluated (criterion represents a single guideline).

criterion-referenced test. A test in which a student's performance is measured relative to explicit learning tasks (usually locally defined) serving as criteria rather than according to norms set in test standardization. For example, a road test for a driver's license represents a criterion-referenced test.

critical thinking. Thinking with special attention to the validity of premises and evidence and careful application of logic.

criticism. 1. Interpretation and evaluation of literary or other artistic endeavors. Favorable evaluation is called "positive" criticism;

unfavorable evaluation, "negative" criticism; and evaluation with suggestions for improvement offered, "constructive" criticism. 2. Commonly, unfavorable judgments.

critique. A discursive analysis or a knowledgeable and critical examination, discussion, and review of a work, topic, or performance; students are asked frequently to present critiques in literature, art, and music classes.

cross-cultural studies. Systematic efforts to study and compare psychological, sociological, and anthropological aspects of different cultural groups, and to derive conclusions based upon such study.

cross grade-level grouping. See banding.

cross-reference. A notation in a publication for the reader to consult another section for related or supplementary information.

cultural bias. Inclination to discriminate tacitly or overtly against a particular cultural group, usually a minority group, or some aspect of the group such as its interests, values, or worth.

cultural gap. See culture lag.

culturally deprived child. See culturally disadvantaged child.

culturally disadvantaged child. A child whose community or social setting lacks means for becoming familiar with cultural activities such as painting and sculpture, classical music, and drama.

culture lag. Failure of one sector of a culture or society to keep up with the development of other sectors of the culture; or failure of a whole culture to keep up with the development of another culture or cultures. Also called cultural gap.

culture shock. A psychological reaction experienced by some people upon encountering a new and different society or way of life; characterized by uncertainty and anxiety.

cum laude. Latin term meaning "with distinction"; used to denote high scholastic achievement by a higher-education graduating student and so indicated on the student's degree. Three levels of cum laude graduation awards are cum laude, magna cum laude (with great distinction), and summa cum laude (with greatest distinction). Sometimes also awarded to secondary school graduates.

cumulative average. Most often, the average of the course grades received by a student in secondary or higher education, from the beginning of high school, or of college, or of graduate school. See grade-point average.

current events. Customary term for a learning activity in school based upon news events in economics, politics, social life, art, science, and other fields, presented to students as topics for discussion, usually in social studies classes.

curriculum. 1. The entire program of studies offered in a school, college or other educational institution. 2. The program of courses of a particular kind that is offered by an institution, such as the curriculum for the bachelor's degree in mechanical engineering, or the institution's several curricula in engineering.

curriculum development. Work aimed at improving or adding to an institution's curriculum, ideally by researching, analyzing, and testing current instruction techniques and objectives as well as introducing guidelines for new curricula.

curriculum enrichment. A process of selectively augmenting a curriculum by adding educational content and new opportunities for learning such as audiovisual presentations, school trips, and guest lecturers.

curriculum evaluation. An appraisal by experienced educators of the current curriculum for purposes of assessing such factors as value of content, effectiveness of learning, validity of objectives, and achievement of goals.

curriculum vitae. See résumé.

curve. See normal distribution curve.

custodian. A skilled building superintendent responsible for all the physical maintenance of the institution's buildings and grounds. Formerly termed janitor.

cutting score. A selected point on a score scale that rigidly divides students attaining scores above and below it into two groups for designated purposes such as admittance or rejection, and pass or fail; testing specialists advise against making enlightened decisions on the basis of a cutting score.

D

D. See grading system.

D. Abbreviation for "Doctor of" when used as the terminating letter in abbreviations for various types of doctor's degrees, as in M.D. and Ph.D. (or in some cases signifies "Doctor of" when used as the initial letter, as in D.D.S. for Doctor of Dental Science).

DAT. See Dental Aptitude Test, Differential Aptitude Tests.

day-care center. A public or private facility providing part-time or full-day custody of preschool children by skilled or semiskilled staff members who usually also provide some teaching. Also called child-care center.

day school. A school to which students travel daily while living at their homes, as opposed to a boarding school where students reside during school terms.

D.D.S. See Doctor of Dental Science.

dean. In higher education, a senior officer who is typically responsible under the president for the operation of the academic program, enforcement of student rules and regulations, and supervision of the faculty and of student services; usually an appointive and tenured position.

dean of students. A college administrative officer responsible for the supervision of all aspects of student life, including housing, campus activities, part-time employment, counseling, placement, and other student personnel services.

dean's list. A list compiled each term by the office of a dean at a college or university and naming the students who have achieved a high grade-point average, usually between 90–100. Equivalent to the honor roll in secondary school.

debate club, debate society. An extracurricular activity or club at a secondary school or college in which students learn and practice organized debating, in debate competition with teams of fellow students and teams from other institutions; a faculty member usually serves as adviser or coach. In some cases called forensic club.

debt limit. See bonding limits.

decentralized administration. An administrative system in a school district in which there is sharing and delegation of decision-making and control by subunits, each having jurisdiction over a particular school or function.

decile. A unit in a ten-unit scale, on which rank-order standings of students according to indices such as grades or test scores may be given as standings by decile or tenth; for instance, a student in the top 10% in some respect like class rank stands in the top decile.

deductive reasoning. Drawing logical inferences from general principles for application to particular instances; for example, "All cows give milk; therefore, this brown cow gives milk."

defense mechanism. A behavioral pattern that serves to protect an individual against threats to physical safety, emotional equilibrium, or general well-being, by using such behavioral techniques as rationalization, altered perception, self-deception, or attack on the threatening party.

defense of the thesis. See orals.

degree. An academic title given by a college or university to an individual who has successfully completed a program of studies that fulfill the requirements for graduation and the degree. See associate degree, bachelor's degree, doctor's degree, master's degree.

degree requirements. Specifications of minimum courses, course distribution in a curriculum, and grades required for a degree in higher education in a particular field of study.

Degrees of Reading Power (DRP). See reading power.

delinquent child. A school-age child who violates the rules of the school or who breaks the law; may be dealt with by school or police authorities, depending upon the seriousness of the infraction. See juvenile delinquent.

demography. The scientific study of the characteristics of human populations, and applications of it; demographic analyses are especially important in planning for new public schools.

demonstration center. Educational facilities or classrooms organized to demonstrate an effective educational approach, as with a demonstration school.

demonstration school. 1. A school operated to provide a model educational facility applying practices that merit widespread adoption. 2. In teacher education, a school that demonstrates teaching methods primarily for observation by students preparing to become teachers.

Dental Aptitude Test (DAT). A test widely required for admission to dentistry doctorate schools in the United States; among qualities it examines are scientific aptitude and perceptual and motor abilities.

department. 1. In institutions of higher education and secondary schools, a basic organizational unit consisting of all the faculty members or teaching personnel in a given subject-matter field or academic discipline, such as the department of physics, the department of English, or the department of economics. 2. A nonfaculty organizational unit of an educational institution, like the department of buildings and grounds.

departmentalization. The educational practice in which each teacher provides instruction in one particular subject, and the students move to the classrooms of individual teachers in successive class periods; contrasts with elementary school practice, in which the same teacher instructs the same class in a number of subjects. Departmentalization enables teachers to specialize in subjects and typically marks the start of secondary or early secondary education (in grades 6, 7, 8, or 9).

deprived child. See disadvantaged child.

deschooling. A theory, narrowly held, that schools are inadequate institutions for effective learning, and should be replaced by more individual and self-help faculties such as tutors, libraries, discussion groups, life experience, and other forms of informal learning. Ivan Ilich originated the term, deschooling, with his book *Deschooling Society* (1971).

desegregation. See integration.

detention. A form of punishment consisting of student confinement after school hours to a detention room to do prescribed work for a specific number of days commensurate with his or her offense.

development officer. An administrative officer at an institution of higher education who is responsible for its fund-raising, and in some cases is also responsible for the public relations activities associated with fund-raising.

development studies. In higher education, the study of issues and problems of the political, economic, and social growth in developing countries.

Dewey, John (1859-1952). Early twentieth-century educator and major philosopher widely known for his philosophic theories advocating that education play a central role in furthering democracy.

The School and Society (1899, rev. 1915) and *Democracy and Education* (1916) are representative of his educational thought. He was a founder and leader of the "progressive education" movement.

diagnostic guidance technique. Analytic method used by a qualified guidance counselor; draws on biographical records, diagnostic tests, and interviews for information helpful in advising a student about objectives and goals.

diagnostic-prescriptive teaching (DPT). An individualized method of teaching that identifies weaknesses, prescribes learning activities to correct these weaknesses, and subsequently tests students to check their improvement. Pretests (before instruction) and posttests (after instruction) assess student progress.

diagnostic test. 1. Primarily, a type of achievement test in a specific subject with relatively narrow and detailed coverage so that the specific learning needs of individual pupils in that subject may be indicated and met through regular classroom work or remediation. **2.** Loosely, a personality test given to a student by a guidance counselor for diagnostic purposes and possible referral of the student to qualified specialists in mental health.

didactic method. A teaching method that focuses on discipline, conformity, rules, principles, and upright conduct for the learner.

Differential Aptitude Tests (DAT). A set of standardized tests widely used for career and educational counseling, particularly in secondary schools; among areas in which its constituent tests assess aptitudes are verbal reasoning, numerical ability, mechanical reasoning, clerical speed and accuracy, spelling, and perception of spatial relations.

differential growth. Observable variations in the rates and times at which developmental changes occur among young people of comparable age.

diploma. 1. An official document earned by a student upon graduation from primary or secondary school, certifying successful completion of curriculum requirements. 2. A certificate indicating that some specified program of study has been successfully completed.

direct method. A method of teaching a foreign language in which the teacher conducts the class exclusively in that foreign language. Emphasis is on learning to think in the foreign language, and on practice and comprehension in conversation, rather than on formal grammar.

director, directress. Title for the chief administrator, or head teacher usually at a small private school, such as the directress of a Montessori school.

disadvantaged child. A child whose pattern of living lacks sufficiently favorable economic and social conditions to foster his or her normal development, and who subsists at very low levels of living. Minority-group children are in many cases judged to be disadvantaged because of ethnic or racial discrimination. Also termed an underprivileged or deprived child.

discipline. 1. A subject or domain of knowledge such as mathematics; called an academic discipline. 2. Methods used by teachers to bring about student conduct orderly enough for productive learning. 3. A form of teacher classroom direction that is strict and authoritative, designed to bring about student behavior that is submissive and controlled.

disciplinarian. One who attempts to control others by enforcing order, advocating conformity, and demanding obedience to rules and regulations.

discovery method. A teaching technique whereby the student "discovers" independently by experimentation and exploration that which is to be learned, instead of being directly presented with the material to be learned. Similar to heuristic learning.

discrimination. 1. Action based on racial, religious, ethnic, or sexual prejudice. 2. Perception of fine distinctions or differences. 3. In testing, the technical quality of a test to provide results which effectively differentiate between test-takers with respect to the abilities assessed by the test.

displaced aggression. Hostile and aggressive behavior directed toward a person or object bearing no relation to the cause of those feelings but serving as a target. For example, an older girl physically abusing a younger brother upon learning she failed a test.

dissertation. In higher education, a required treatise or thesis usually based upon original research and written by a candidate at the end of a program of study leading to the Ph.D. and some other types of doctoral degrees. Must be approved and accepted by the candidate's dissertation advisor, and defended orally by the candidate before the doctoral degree is conferred.

distinguished professor. Title in higher education to signify stature and rank of a faculty member above that of professor; customarily reserved for individuals of special eminence.

distractor. In psychological testing, an incorrect alternative among the choices of answers given after a question on a multiple-choice test. See multiple-choice test.

distributive education. Obsolescent term for vocational education and training for students of 14 years of age and older, in preparation for occupations in retailing and marketing.

district superintendent. See superintendent of schools.

district supervisor. See supervisor.

disturbed child. A child with emotional difficulties stemming from organic or functional disorders, which interfere with normal learning and usually cause behavior problems in school. Also called emotionally disturbed.

divergent thinking. Description of an individual's mental activity that tends to answer questions and analyze problems by using intellectual approaches that may be unconventional, untried, innovative, creative, and that look for possible multiple answers and solutions; the opposite of convergent thinking.

divinity school. See theological school.

division. See lower division, upper division.

doctoral degree, doctorate. The highest earned degree awarded for higher education studies; normally takes at least three or four years of full-time study beyond the bachelor's degree to earn. Also called doctor's degree. See "Doctor of" entries for major types of doctorates.

Doctor of Dental Science (D.D.S.). One of the major types of doctor's degree awarded by graduate schools of dentistry (and normally requiring four years of full-time study); an equivalent degree is Doctor of Dental Surgery (also D.D.S.). Such a degree is one of the requirements for admission to the profession of dentistry.

Doctor of Education (Ed.D.). A degree on the level of the Doctor of Philosophy degree awarded for graduate study in an area of professional teacher education; for the Ed.D., dissertation requirements commonly used for the Ph.D. may be replaced by requirements for an extensive field study or developmental project with appropriate reports.

Doctor of Jurisprudence (J.D.). 1. The academic degree predominantly awarded on completion of the regular graduate study program of law schools in the United States (such completion normally requires full-time study for three academic years); such a law-school degree is required (with subsequent passing of the state bar examination) in order to become an attorney. 2. The law-school graduation degree that is currently the equivalent to the Bachelor of Laws (LL.B.), the degree most widely awarded by law schools in previous decades.

Doctor of Medicine (M.D.). The degree awarded on graduation from a medical school after completing general education for the profession of physician; see medical school.

Doctor of Philosophy (Ph.D.). The type of earned doctorate normally awarded in one of the academic disciplines or fields of the humanities, social sciences, or sciences; typical Ph.D. requirements include at least two years of full-time study beyond the bachelor's and a doctoral dissertation embodying original research.

doctor's degree. See doctoral degree.

dogmatic. In teaching, a style characterized by assertive, absolute authoritarian instruction, allowing for little questioning or challenge by students.

dormitory. Residence hall for boarding students in a school or college; may include dining and recreational facilities.

double major. In higher education, carrying out major concentrations of study in two areas rather than only in one, as with a double major in English and history. See major.

double sessions. Emergency type of student attendance schedule adopted by a school enabling it to accommodate physically up to twice the normal enrollment; such a schedule includes an extended morning session attended by one group of students, and an extended afternoon session attended by a completely different group of students. For any one student, either the morning session or the afternoon session constitutes the entire school day. Also called split sessions.

DPT. See diagnostic-prescriptive teaching.

dress code. Regulations of a school or college governing ways in which students must be dressed; such codes tended to be adopted with some frequency in the counterculture years of the 1960s.

drill. 1. A teaching method used to insure thoroughness of learning by repetitious practice in an activity. 2. Formerly, the name for training in physical education.

drive. Motivated, energetic behavior directed toward a goal, as with the drive to achieve high grades.

driver education. In secondary school, a one-term course of class-room and on-the-road instruction in safe automobile driving and preparation for driver-license tests.

drop-out. 1. A student who leaves the formal education system before completing studies required for a high-school diploma or a college degree, thereby forfeiting graduation. Usually a drop-out may resume studies for graduation at the same or a different school at a later date. **2.** drop-out or dropout: In programmed instruction, a section of the material to be learned that is removed from further practice when the student answers the questions correctly in that particular section. The drop-out device enables students to practice in sections that need improvement.

DRP. See reading power.

drug abuse education. Instruction in separate courses or as part of courses in health about the effects and dangers of taking illicit drugs such as marijuana, heroin, or cocaine; courses may be given in secondary schools or colleges.

dual-control car. A frequent safety feature in driver education, representing an auto equipped with two sets of controls so that either the student-driver or the instructor may control the car.

dyslexia. A reading disability apparently caused by a neurological dysfunction in which the student experiences difficulty in clearly perceiving individual letters, words, or passages. Dyslexic students often need special instructional provisions and may ultimately outgrow or overcome the handicap.

E

early admission. Usually the formal acceptance of an applicant into a college or university before the student has completed the last year or semester of secondary studies, resulting in high-school acceleration of the applicant.

early childhood. A child's beginning years, from infancy to about the age of nine years. Important in educational psychology as a subject for coursework and research.

early childhood education. Schooling and activities related to the development of children from birth through grade 3; includes nursery school, kindergarten, and grades 1 through 3.

early decision plan. A plan adopted as part of the admissions policy of a college under which an applicant can receive the college's decision on admission early in the high school senior year instead of at the end of the senior year. Typically, in such a plan the student must apply by a deadline early in the fall of the senior year. The student agrees to accept admission if it is offered, the college reports its decision to admit or not by a date in December of the student's senior year, and the student if rejected may opt to have his or her application considered without prejudice on the regular admissions schedule. Colleges with early decision plans subscribe to the Candidates Reply Date Agreement. See Candidates Reply Date Agreement, early admission, rolling admission.

early intervention. Any effort to provide compensatory education to disadvantaged children at an early age; a term given currency in the 1960s.

72

ecology. 1. The specialized branch of the biological sciences treating the interactions between living creatures and their environments. 2. In loose references by environmentalists in recent decades, the wholesome totality of mutually dependent relationships between living creatures and their environments when left in the natural state.

Economic Opportunity Act of 1964. A federal law passed by Congress in 1964 with sections relevant to education: Title I established the Job Corps for disadvantaged youth needing employment; Title II provided for urban and rural community action programs for low-income individuals and families to attain skills; Title VIII established a domestic volunteer program. Incorporated into CETA in 1973. See Comprehensive Education and Training Act, Job Corps program, VISTA.

economics. The study of the production, distribution, consumption, and exchange of goods and services derived from natural resources and labor and involving monetary values.

Ed.D. See Doctor of Education degree.

educable mentally retarded. See mentally retarded.

education. 1. Any process, formal or informal, that helps develop the potentialities of human beings, including their knowledge, capabilities, behavior patterns, and values. 2. The developmental process provided by a school or other institution that is organized chiefly for instruction and learning. 3. The total development acquired by an individual through instruction and learning. 4. In business or official connections, the institutional instruction that the individual has had. 5. The area of study concerned with teaching and learning, including professional teacher education.

educational administration. In professional teacher education, the study of planning, organizing, directing, and managing the human and material resources and systems in an educational institution.

educational assessment. The analysis and evaluation of the accomplishments of current educational objectives of an institution or program for purposes of future curriculum development, planning, policy-making, and resource allocation.

educational broker. A projected variety of educational specialist who acts as an intermediary between adult learners and educational resources. Broker functions include providing information, counseling, recommendations, and client assessment for a fee.

educational consultant. A professional specialist in particular areas of education who advises educational administrators, corporations, or other organizations or individuals drawing on the consultant's services.

educational corporation. A nonprofit organization or association that is chartered under state law as a corporation for educational purposes (usually, not including schools, colleges, or foundations); among examples are The College Board, and Educational Testing Service.

educational deferment. Term used when a military draft is in force for the temporary postponement for drafted students of their military service until they complete their higher or professional education.

educational employee benefits. Fringe benefits provided employees in the area of education, including eligibility of employee children in scholarship programs sponsored by the employers, tuition refund programs for college courses taken by employees, and other education and training provided or funded for employees by the employers.

educational endowment. See endowment.

educational hierarchy. In an educational system, the formal administrative structure of authority in which control and responsibility are highest at the top and lesser as ranks descend.

educational measurement. See measurement.

educational mobility. **1.** The quality of an educational system permitting individuals to move readily between different types of educational programs and institutions in the system. 2. A term sometimes used to mean upward social mobility due to one's education; improvement in an individual's socioeconomic position as a result of formal education.

educational psychology. 1. The study of the nature and operation of the human learning process. 2. The study of the psychological issues and problems directly related to teaching and learning including mental processes, emotions, and behavior.

educational radio station. 1. A radio broadcasting station regularly operated by a college or other educational institution, either as a student activity or an adjunct to instruction. 2. A radio station engaged primarily in educational broadcasting.

Educational Resources Information Center (ERIC). One of several centers in the ERIC computerized information system operated by the National Institute of Education (NIE); data stored and disseminated by the center are drawn from such sources as research studies, curriculum and teaching guides, program evaluations, and instructional materials.

educational television (ETV). 1. In schooling, broadcasts of material in school that supplement or reinforce coursework; programs are noncommercial and may be transmitted by closed-circuit TV. 2. Loosely, television programming used in education.

Educational Testing Service (ETS). A private, nonprofit organization devoted to measurement and research, primarily in education; best known as the agency that gives the tests of The College Board and other tests that have included the Graduate Management Admission Test (GMAT), Law School Admission Test (LMSAT), Graduate Record Examinations (GRE), and National Teacher Examinations. Its main offices are in Princeton, NJ.

educational voucher. See voucher plan.

Education Index. A publication for reference purposes serving as a subject-author-title guide to articles in other periodicals dealing with education; monthly, cumulated annually.

Education of All Handicapped Children Act of 1975. A federal law requiring all public schools to integrate handicapped children with "normal" children in regular classrooms for instruction, in order to increase socialization and develop self-confidence, thereby enhancing learning ability. In order to receive financial aid, the schools are required to devise appropriate Individualized Education Programs (IEPs) for handicapped children in consultation with their parents and arrange for them to be taught alongside their "normal" peers. See mainstream, special education.

educator. A professional practitioner in the field of education, usually engaged in either teaching or administration.

EE. Electrical engineering, the engineering specialty that deals with electrical phenomena; generally considered to have two broad branches, electrical power engineering and electronics engineering.

ego. In popular applications of Freudian psychoanalytic theory, the conscious mind or the self that directs behavior and perceives reality; ego begins to develop during early childhood when the child becomes aware of difference between "I" and "you," or "it."

egocentric. The quality of being self-centered and unresponsive to the needs of others; frequently observed in young children before offset by sufficient socialization and maturation.

elective courses. Courses that students may "elect" (freely choose) to take for credit toward their intended degrees or diplomas — as distinguished from courses that are specifically required.

Elementary and Secondary Education Act of 1965. A federal law passed by Congress in 1965 during Lyndon Johnson's administration to improve educational quality and educational opportunities in elementary and secondary public and nonpublic schools through five titles: Title I authorized $1 billion to improve school programs in low-income areas; Title II authorized $100 million to states for school library resources; Title III authorized $100 million for supplementary educational centers such as mobile libraries, language and science laboratories, and programmed instruction; Title IV authorized $100 million over a five-year period for educational research and training; and Title V authorized $25 million to strengthen state departments of education.

elementary education. The period of formal schooling in the United States beginning with kindergarten (noted as "K") or first grade through grades 6, 7, or 8, though most school systems today treat grades 6–8 or 7–8 as secondary ones. Elementary curricula begin with reading, writing, and arithmetic, then include simplified material in such subjects as geography, science, and history. Elementary schools may be in buildings housing classes in grades K–5, K–6, K–7, or K–8. An elementary school is sometimes called a grade school.

elementary school. See elementary education.

elhi. A term used in the field of textbook publishing to refer to functions, departments, and other matters concerned with learning materials for elementary schools and high schools.

Emergency Employment Act. A federal law enacted by Congress in 1972 to eliminate overlapping federal funding for programs. Led to the passage of CETA and incorporated therein. See Comprehensive Education and Training Act.

emerita. Feminine form of emeritus; see emeritus.

emeritus. An honorary title in higher education conferred on faculty members or administrators after their retirement, as in professor emeritus or dean emeritus.

emotional adjustment. 1. The process by which one deals with and manages one's feelings with respect to internal and external stimuli, within the capabilities of one's psychological framework. 2. The result of applying this process.

emotional instability. 1. An emotional condition characterized by wide fluctuations in mood. 2. The inability to control one's emotions.

emotionally disturbed child. See disturbed child.

emotional maturity. In an individual, the quality of having reasonable stability in feelings and balance in moods as exhibited by normal adults.

empathy. 1. Identification with the feelings of another and comprehension of those feelings without experiencing the feelings subjectively. **2.** A sense of such indentification when experiencing a work of art.

empirical. A term describing knowledge that is based upon observation, experiment, or experience, rather than on theory.

employee education. Programs of education and training offered by many larger corporations and government agencies for their employees; courses offered in such programs may range from basic instruction in office procedures and skills or technical processes to postdoctoral-level study for scientists and engineers.

encyclopedia. 1. Reference work containing many entries on individual topics drawn from almost all fields of knowledge, with entries usually presented alphabetically. **2.** Such a work comprehensively treating one field of knowledge; also called a cyclopedia.

endowment. A fund intended to be permanently held by an institution in at least its original amount and devoted to general or specified purposes. The principal is invested, while the income earned as interest is used for the stated purposes.

engineering technology. The fields of instruction in engineering specialties preparing persons for paraprofessional careers as engineering technicians (in specialties such as electrical engineering technicians, mechanical engineering technicians, and chemical engineering technicians); engineering technology programs are often ones taking two years of full-time study to complete and leading to the degree of associate in applied science.

English. General term for the very broad area of study in education concerned with the English language. See also American English, black English, Standard English.

English as a Second Language (ESL). The field of teaching Standard English as used in the United States to persons who have a different native language; ESL courses are widely offered for foreign students and in programs of bilingual education.

English composition. See composition.

enrichment program. A program with scope that goes beyond the normal educational content of a course of study, and that is fuller and broader for students of high academic ability.

enrollment. 1. The entering of one's name as a student in the official register of a school, other educational institution, program, or course. 2. The total number of persons registered as students in any given educational entity such as a school, school district, course, or class at a given time.

entrance examination. Older term for admissions test. See admissions test.

environment. 1. The totality of external surroundings, including conditions, circumstances, and events; in education, often considered for the extent to which such surroundings facilitate or impede learning. 2. The natural environment as generally viewed by the environmentalist movement prominent in the United States beginning in the 1960s.

environmental studies. In higher or secondary education, an interdisciplinary course or program of study and research drawing on such areas as ecology and other biological sciences, the earth sciences, economics, and political science.

equality of educational opportunity. In an educational system, the offering of the same or comparable opportunities for study and educational improvement to all individuals, without regard to race, religion, ethnic background, or economic status.

equalization aid. See federal equalization aid.

equation. 1. In mathematics, an expression in symbols and numerals stating the equality of two quantities and using the = (equals) sign between them. 2. In chemistry, an expression in symbols and numbers representing a chemical reaction.

equivalency tests. 1. Tests for the high-school diploma enabling persons to earn the diploma after having missed the chance to complete coursework for it. 2. Any examinations to assess the extent to which an individual's knowledge fulfills some specific program requirements of a school or college.

ERIC. See Educational Resources Information Center.

Erickson, Erik (1902–). German-born psychologist, specializing in the study of child and adolescent psychology, and originator of a widely influential theory of the life cycle in human development. See identity crisis.

error of measurement. In testing theory, the extent to which any actual score earned by an individual on a test can vary from the individual's theoretical true score on the test simply because of chance factors. The form of this error termed the standard error of measurement relates the error to the standard deviation for the test. The error of measurement inherent in any test leads testing specialists to urge that any individual's scores on a test be viewed as only tentative and approximate findings rather than as precise and conclusive.

ESEA. See Elementary and Secondary Education Act of 1965.

ESL. See English as a Second Language.

essay. 1. In literature, an interpretive or analytical prose composition of relatively short length; the form of writing predominantly used for literary criticism. 2. A composition or paper written as a course assignment by a student. See also essay test.

essay test. Test or examination in which the individual is required to provide answers in the form of one or more written essays; contrasts with such types of short-answer tests as multiple-choice, true-false, or sentence-completion. See essay.

essentialism. A lesser-known educational theory that there exists a body of fundamental knowledge, skill, and ideals, with implied high standards of attainment, which should be taught to all students.

establishment. 1. Phrased as "the establishment," term that gained wide currency among students in the 1960s to signify all sectors of American society perpetuating the status quo. 2. Traditionally, as in "the establishment."

ethics. 1. A branch of philosophy dealing with the moral nature of human conduct. 2. The principles and standards guiding upright moral conduct in everyday life or in a special field or profession.

ethnic group. A distinct cultural and social subgroup within a larger culture, often distinguished by background in a particular national tradition, language, religion, or race.

ethnography. See anthropology.

ethnology. See anthropology.

ETS. See Educational Testing Service.

ETV. See educational television.

evaluation. In education generally, an assessment or appraisal of any appropriate entity and expressed descriptively or numerically.

evening school. 1. Older term for any program of courses scheduled on weekday evenings; also called night school. 2. Older term for an adjunct of a secondary school offering academic vocational training, and recreational instruction for adults and young people employed through weekday hours.

examination. 1. In education, a test or assessment of learning through the use of questions devised by qualified educators. 2. Any systematic inspection or test.

exceptional child. 1. A child below average in measured mental, physical, or emotional ability who requires special education guided by special education teachers in order to realize his or her potential. Sometimes referred to as a "slow learner" or "handicapped" pupil. 2. A child well above average in measured mental or physical ability who often requires intensification, enrichment, and acceleration in learning in order to realize his or her potential. Sometimes called a "gifted child."

exchange students. Students in higher education or secondary education who come to the United States from foreign countries, and counterpart American students who go to their countries, under agreements between governments or groups in the respective countries for such mutual exchange of students; an exchange student typically goes abroad for one academic year.

exchange teachers. Teachers or professors who come to the United States from foreign countries, and counterpart American teachers or professors who go to their countries, under agreements between governments or groups in the respective countries for such mutual exchange; exchange assignments often run for one academic year and can include teaching, writing, lecturing, or research.

excused absence. Legal nonattendance of school for reasons of personal or family illness, death of a relative, or religious or personal obligations.

exercise. 1. In education, a ceremony or formal assembly to mark an occasion such as opening of the school year or graduation; often called exercises. 2. A problem or task for the student to work in practice, an assignment, or textbook study. **3.** Physical activity for body development and fitness. **4.** In general, to use or make use of.

expectancy table. A numerical table concerning a designated group of individuals that one may consult to find out, for the standing of an individual in the group on one variable (like a test score), what future outcome can be expected for that individual in terms of another variable (like freshman-year grade-point average) and, preferably, expected with what degree of probability.

expenditure per student. The annual expense per student incurred by one or more educational institutions in providing education; regarded by some as a relative indicator of the quality of education.

experiential learning. 1. In theories of learning and educational philosophy, one major mode of acquiring knowledge, through experience, as illustrated by student laboratory experiments in the sciences. **2.** In the lifelong learning movement originating in the 1970s, college-level learning acquired by adults in their work or cultural activities; many colleges systematically evaluate such learning for degree credit and award credit as warranted. This practice is sometimes loosely referred to as the award of "life-experience credit."

experiment. 1. In science, a laboratory operation designed and carried out to provide new data as evidence tending to confirm or invalidate a scientific hypothesis. **2.** Generally, a trial or test of something new.

experimental college. An institution of higher education with nontraditional and innovative curricula, teaching methods, policies, and procedures.

experimental method. Broadly, the methods of discovering and validating knowledge through observation and experiment, as in the sciences.

experimental school. School with a nontraditional and innovative curriculum, teaching methods, and educational philosophy.

expulsion. The discharge of a student from the school ordered by school authorities, as a disciplinary act and punishment for extremely serious misbehavior and usually only after repeated warnings. The student is usually barred permanently from that particular school following expulsion. See suspension.

extended family. All of the individual's blood relations extending beyond the basic conjugal family unit of father, mother, and children; includes such relatives as grandparents, aunts, uncles, nieces, nephews, and cousins.

extended school day. A lengthened schedule of operation which increases the hours a day that a school is in session to accommodate students for academic, recreational, or compensatory purposes.

extension agent. One of numerous officers holding dual appointments with the United States Department of Agriculture and land-grant universities who provide community services primarily in agricultural and rural areas; types of agents include the agricultural agent, the home demonstration agent, and the Four-H Club agent. See land-grant institutions.

extension center. An off-campus, branch facility of a college or university where part-time students can take courses at locations selected as especially accessible to such students.

extension education. 1. Older term for programs of part-time, evening courses offered by universities and colleges primarily for adults either in degree-credit areas or in noncredit areas for career development or cultural enrichment purposes; in current years, often called continuing education and offered by a university's school of continuing education. 2. Educational services offered by extension agents on the staffs of land-grant universities and colleges. See extension agent.

extension studies. 1. Obsolescent term in adult education referring to instructional activities provided by a university or college for people who are not a part of the usual student body. May be given off-campus, evenings, or weekends. Work may go beyond the normal range of subject areas or be interdisciplinary. 2. See extension agent.

external degree programs. 1. Higher education programs in which individuals may carry out all learning and meet all other requirements for academic degrees with no attendance at course sessions and no following of any required schedules; much or all degree credit in such programs may be earned through credit by examination. **2.** Loosely, similar programs that require relatively little attendance for instruction or guidance.

external examination. 1. A test administered by a school or college to an individual who is not a student at the institution, but who is completing a course of study independently or at another institution. **2.** In general, examinations for students that originate outside the institution or institutions they attend.

extra-class activities. See extracurricular activities.

extracurricular activities. Academic or nonacademic functions engaged in by students outside of and in addition to courses of study, such as athletic teams, journalistic or literary publications, dramatic or debating or campus service societies, and student government bodies, all under the auspices of the school or college. Sometimes called extra-class activities, but extra-class activities usually denote activities which supplement courses of study such as a trip to the Museum of Natural History for social studies, or a visit to a theater for English drama.

eye fixations. In reading, the actions of the reader in which the sweeping motion of the eyes is stopped and the eyes examine a group of letters or words to register their meaning; most of the reading time is occupied by such fixations.

eye regressions. In reading, the actions of the reader in which the eyes are moved back to a passage earlier scanned because the meaning of the passage has not been grasped; such regressions greatly slow reading speed.

F

F. See grading system.

faculty. 1. The entire staff of professional teachers and research scholars at an institution of higher education or secondary education. **2.** In some cases, the entire staff of professional educators at an institution, including administrators. **3.** The professional teaching staff of a department or other division of an institution, like the faculty of music or faculty of medicine; in past centuries, this use of the term faculty also often referred to the division itself. **4.** Generally, a capability of an individual.

faculty advisor. In higher education, a staff member who helps students with academic matters like the selection of courses, requirements, and registration, and who provides other academic information pertinent to the student's needs.

faculty-student ratio. Customarily given in the form of student-faculty ratio. See student-teacher ratio.

FAF. See Financial Aid Form.

failing grade. 1. A mark denoting individual scholastic achievement that falls below minimally acceptable standards; as a final course grade, it means that the student receives no credit for the course. **2.** Individual performance that does not successfully meet the required passing grade in an examination or other activity assessed by grades. See grading system, pass.

fallacy. 1. A false statement or idea based upon incorrect reasoning. 2. Mistaken and deceptive reasoning that leads to incorrect conclusions.

Family Educational Rights and Privacy Act. A federal statute adopted in 1974 that gives students or the parents of students who are minors the right to review the student's records on file at any school, college, or other educational institution; it provides that federal funds will be denied to any institution that refuses to open such records to the student or parent. It similarly requires authorization by the student or parent of release of any part of such records to an outside party. The law was enacted as an amendment to the Elementary and Secondary School Act of 1974; it is at times referred to as the Buckley Amendment because it was sponsored by James L. Buckley, then a senator from New York.

Family Financial Statement (FFS). Blank form which colleges require applicants for financial aid to complete; similar in character and purpose to the Financial Aid Form, but sponsored by the American College Testing Program. See Financial Aid Form.

family grouping. See nongraded class.

family life education. 1. Education at any level of schooling designed to provide students with knowledge regarding successful family living in terms of human behavior, emotional maturity, social skills, and group involvement. 2. Education on the secondary or college level designed to prepare students for successful interpersonal relationships, marriage, sexual relations, home management, and parenthood.

family planning. See birth control.

federal aid to education. Monetary funds in the form of grants and appropriations given by the United States government to educational institutions through states and local authorities to implement educational programs with varying degrees of federal control in the programs. Amounts of funds vary with different presidential administrations.

federal equalization aid. A term for hypothetical federal funds that might be distributed to help needy school districts attain a minimal, satisfactory level of education, based upon standards of national comparison.

feedback. 1. Figurative term for the responses or reactions to an action that can enable the initiator of the action to improve the effectiveness of the action on repeated tries; prompt feedback in this sense from a teacher to students is thought to facilitate the students' learning. **2.** In programmed instruction, information received by the student (also called reinforcement) immediately after a response to a programmed step; in programmed instruction, the student is given a small step of new information to learn, is questioned on the step for a response, and after the student's answer is given the correct answer is provided as immediate "feedback" or reinforcement. See programmed instruction.

fellow. 1. A member of a learned society. **2.** A graduate student holding a financial aid grant called a fellowship. **3.** A senior member of a professional institution.

fellowship. A grant of financial aid held by a graduate student.

FFS. See Family Financial Statement.

field. 1. A study area in which the student can major for a degree; see major. **2.** Any area of activity, interest, or endeavor, business, or profession. **3.** The setting or environment within which events occur or people interact.

field day. A special function in which a school or college holds outdoor activities such as competitive athletics and recreational sports supervised by coaches and other school personnel.

field study. In higher education, research carried out away from the institution and in direct contact with the people, natural phenomena, or other entities being studied; especially frequent in fields including anthropology, archaeology, sociology, earth sciences, and environmental studies. Also called field work.

field trip. Planned visit by a group of students and teachers to a site of specific or general pertinence to some aspect of the students' learning, such as an art museum, historic landmark, newspaper office, or manufacturing plant.

field work. See field study.

final, finals. See final examination.

final examination. Examination given at the end of a course; typically covers all the work in the course, is longer and harder than periodic course tests, and counts heavily in the final course grade. Also instantly recognized among students when called by the informal name, "final" or "finals."

financial aid. **1.** Student financial aid consists of funds in such varied forms as scholarships, grants, interest-subsidized loans, campus employment, fellowships, and assistantships that are provided for students in higher education (or, to a lesser extent, for students in private schools) to assist the students in paying their educational costs (including tuition, room and board, and books and supplies). **2.** Institutional financial aid consists of funds provided educational institutions or public school districts to assist with their financing; such institutional aid is supplied chiefly by federal or state governments, but may also be furnished by foundations or other philanthropic bodies.

Financial Aid Form (FAF). Blank form on which colleges require applicants for financial aid to provide detailed information in confidence on the family's finances; with the information, the college can evaluate how much the family can reasonably and justly afford toward college costs, which enables the college to adjust the amount of financial aid it offers a student according to need. The FAF is sponsored by the College Scholarship Service (CSS) of The College Board.

financial aid officer. A relatively new type of administrative officer at an institution of higher education who is responsible for extensive operations related to student financial aid.

financial aid package. The combination of forms of financial aid and amounts in each form that is offered an individual student. See financial aid.

financial need. 1. In student financial aid for college, the difference between the student's annual college costs at a specific college and the annual amount the student (and the student's family) can reasonably afford to spend for college expenses as estimated in a need analysis system. **2.** Generally, the state of insufficient financial resources for living at a subsistence level.

fine arts. Fields of the arts characterized purely or predominantly by aesthetics, in contrast to applied arts that substantially involve practical or commercial considerations. Fine arts fields chiefly include painting, sculpture, music, dance, drama, and architecture. See also studio art.

finger math. An extensively developed system for rapidly carrying out complex arithmetic calculations using only the fingers; it is taught as suplementary learning in the early grades in some schools to help develop confidence and familiarity with numbers.

fire drill. A required periodic activity in elementary and secondary schools consisting of practice steps to be taken in the event of a fire; results in the evacuation of people from the buildings after the sounding of school fire alarms.

flash cards. Cards individually giving a fact, term, or anything else to be learned so that a teacher or learner can hold each card for viewing and memorization in turn; widely used as a teaching aid with young children being introduced to reading and arithmetic, and for memorizing and drill in any subject. A variant form for drill poses a question on one side and answers it on the other.

FLES. Acronym for Foreign Language in Elementary School, an effort of some prominence in the 1960s to encourage the teaching of foreign languages in American elementary schools.

flexible progression. Term loosely applied to a teaching practice in which students in a class or course are allowed to progress through the subject matter at their own individual rates.

flexible scheduling. Flexibility rather than uniformity on the part of a school in setting the regular times for the meeting of courses and classes, with such flexibility provided to meet the needs of special activities or instructional approaches.

fluency. 1. Facility in speaking a language rapidly and correctly, and often also in writing and reading it. **2.** Smoothly flowing facility of any kind. **3.** Capability of carrying out any kind of function easily and smoothly.

Follow Through Program. A program introduced in the 1960s for disadvantaged children in grades 1–3 who had previously been in the Head Start Program and designed to reinforce and continue compensatory education for those children; both it and Head Start were first funded through the U.S. Department of Health, Education and Welfare.

flunk. Slang word meaning to fail in taking a test, or in meeting minimum academic requirements in a course or grade.

forced-choice technique. A technique for presenting answers to test questions in which the individual is required to select an answer among options that are generally equally acceptable but unequally valid; often used to assess the individual's powers of discrimination and scrutiny.

forecasting. Predicting future events, outcomes, or trends based upon previous experience or data, current information, and forecasting formulae and techniques.

foreign language house. At some colleges and universities, a building maintained by a foreign language department where students studying the language may meet other students, faculty members, and native speakers and join in programs on the language and culture of the country.

foreign student. A student from one country who is studying in another country, usually on the level of secondary or higher education. Also called international student.

forensic club. See debate club, debate society.

formal education. Education in recognized educational institutions, as distinguished from what one has learned outside schools and colleges.

formative evaluation. Term used at times to refer to an appraisal by school authorities based on test scores and other data to help ascertain the extent to which future school programs, curriculum, and activities need to be modified or improved to maintain standards.

formula. 1. In mathematics, a rule or principle usually stated in mathematical notation, like the formula for the area of a rectangle. 2. In chemistry, an expression in symbolic notation for the number of each kind of atom in a substance, such as H_2O (empirical formula), or a similar diagrammatic expression also indicating links between atoms (structural formula). 3. A prescription or recipe, as with infant's milk formula. 4. Any codified statement of a uniform procedure.

foster parent. A man or woman who, in the absence of the child's corresponding biological parent, legally or practically serves in that parental role.

foundation. Most notably in education, a private philanthropic trust or endowed institution providing grant support; funding from foundations serves many significant purposes in education, including student financial aid, development of needed new programs, and research projects.

foundations of education. Name for a widely offered college course in the philosophy, social forces, history, and psychology upon which the formal educational system is based; required in the professional teacher-education curriculum.

four-year college. College offering a substantial range of study programs leading to bachelor's degrees (normally completed in full-time study for four academic years, but which the college may offer in ways permitting completion in a fewer or greater number of years); a four-year college may also offer some associate-degree and graduate-degree programs. See bachelor's degree.

fraternity. A collegiate club or society for male students, usually part of a national group and serving social purposes. Referred to by Greek letters as TKA for Tau Kappa Alpha; frequently maintains a residence or "house" for members, and employs an initiation ceremony for inducting new members. See also honorary fraternity, honorary sorority, Phi Beta Kappa, professional fraternity, sorority.

free period. In secondary school or college, a regularly scheduled class period during which a student or teacher has no regularly assigned class or other commitment.

free play. In nursery school, day care, or kindergarten, a brief period of time during which the child's activities are formally unstructured by the teacher.

frequency distribution. A mathematical property of a set of numerical values such as course grades or test scores of a group of students; pertains to what might be called the proportionate spread of the grades or scores from low through average and high. For example, the familiar bell-shaped curve of normal probability graphs the frequency distribution of such grades or scores if they were to correspond to a theoretically perfect distribution by chance. See normal distribution curve.

freshman. 1. A first-year student matriculated in a four-year college or university. 2. Sometimes refers to a first-year student in a four-year secondary school.

freshman orientation. See orientation program.

Froebel, Friedrich, W. A. (1782-1852). German educator who originated the type of schooling continued today as the kindergarten grade in elementary schooling. Schools he founded included a training college and demonstration school and, after his death, many kindergartens based on his theories were introduced in Europe and the United States.

frustration threshold. A loose term for the level of relative discouragement that an individual can typically tolerate before dropping efforts to reach some goal. Individuals range from low to high in their frustration threshold; children generally start low and move toward the higher range with increasing maturity.

FTE. See full-time equivalents.

Fulbright exchange program. One of the largest official programs of the United States in recent decades to provide for educational exchange internationally; authorized under the Fulbright Act (1946), it provided for extensive exchange of students, teachers, research specialists, and lecturers with counterparts from a number of foreign countries. It was named for James William Fulbright (1905–), U.S. Senator from Arkansas (1945–1975).

full-time. 1. Chiefly in higher education, pertaining to status as a student that represents registration in a full credit load; each institution defines minimum full-time student status in its catalog as registration each term in courses carrying a specified total number of credits, such as 12 semester-hour credits. 2. As applied to years of study in higher education, pertains to the amount of study as measured in total course credits that is completed by typical individuals engaged in full-time studies in the regular academic year; for example, the bachelor's degree is normally earned in four years of full-time study. 3. With reference to faculty members who teach, signifies faculty who are engaged to teach full-time rather than part-time.

full-time equivalents (FTE). 1. In reporting statistics that involve student enrollments in higher education, the number of full-time students that would be equivalent to an actual aggregate of part-time students; for instance, an enrollment of 100 students attending on a quarter-time basis would be reported as an enrollment of 25 full-time equivalents. See full-time. 2. A similar method for converting numbers of part-time teaching faculty to full-time equivalents; provides more meaningful data in calculating such figures as student-faculty ratios.

functional education. Term sometimes applied to courses for which there is immediate practical application, as with courses in mechanical drawing or typing.

functional illiterate. A term used for persons who are unable to read or write at a minimal level for everyday functioning.

functional reading ability. A minimal level of nonacademic reading ability that enables an individual to read practical materials such as signs, simple forms, train schedules, or directions.

fundamentals. **1.** Descriptive term for essential courses that constitute the foundation of learning. **2.** Descriptive term for the basic ideas or structure in any subject or academic discipline.

fused curriculum. In secondary education, a curriculum combining two courses and correlating their subject matter, as in a fused curriculum of literature and history.

G

gaming. Use of simulated situations called "games" in learning and training, especially among business managers and military officers; in the technique, the student is typically required to think critically, take risks, make decisions, and attain specific objectives in managing the situation or task.

general education. 1. A set of courses required by a college for all students and covering what is thought to be the general knowledge important for all educated persons to have; typically includes at least a one-year course each in a subject in the humanities, the social sciences, and the sciences including mathematics, or equivalent interdisciplinary courses. 2. Broadly, the component of an individual's education viewed as needed for general functioning and cultural development, as distinct from specialized studies taken for individual interest and career preparation.

generalization. 1. A statement or conclusion summarizing what is common to a number of detailed observations or facts, reached by reasoning from the particular to the general. 2. The act or process of drawing such a conclusion. 3. A tendency to treat similar instances or events in the same manner.

general science. 1. In early secondary education, a type of course combining study of different major branches of the natural sciences as an introduction to study of the individual branches. 2. Interdisciplinary study of the natural sciences in any level of education from elementary to higher education.

general supervisor. See supervisor.

generation gap. Term widely current in the 1960s referring to an ostensibly unbridgeable gap in communication and understanding between youth and parent generations.

genetics. The biological science of heredity, dealing with the transmission of inherited characteristics by genes.

genius. 1. A person of extremely high talent, and/or superior mental ability demonstrated by exceptional skill, creativity, or accomplishment in a particular field or fields. 2. Extremely high talent of one or more kinds.

geology. The scientific study of the earth, including its history, development, and physical structure.

geometry. A branch of mathematics dealing with points, lines, and figures in space.

geriatrics. Branch of the medical sciences dealing with the elderly.

gerontology. The study of aging and the elderly in fields of the social sciences or sciences.

Gesell, Arnold (1880–1961). American psychologist who, with Frances Ilg, produced research findings and widely influential books on developmental functions that normal infants and children can perform and the normative ages at which they can perform them; the books include *The First Five Years of Life* (1940), *The Child from Five to Ten* (revised 1977), and *Infant and Child in the Culture of Today* (revised 1974).

Gestalt. 1. An informal term referring to the perception of some phenomenon as an organized whole or totality rather than as consisting of various parts. 2. Name of a school of psychological thought developed starting in 1890 which interprets phenomena as organized wholes.

G.I. Bill. Informal term for any of various federal statutes and programs that provided substantial financial benefits for postsecondary and higher education to veterans who had served in the United States Armed Forces in World War II, the Korean War, or the Vietnam War.

gifted child. 1. Among educators, a child whose ability level is far above average, academically, physically, and/or artistically. Gifted children often need specially adapted educational programs for optimum development. 2. Loosely, a child who is born with and demonstrates specific talent in an area, or a child who excels consistently in achievement, either generally or in a specific area.

Girl Scouts. A widely popular organization for girls, similar to the Boy Scouts in its focus on outdoor activities; established in the United States in 1912. See Boy Scouts.

glee club. 1. A student vocal group that tends to perform shorter musical works and specializes in "part" singing. 2. Traditionally, a college vocal group of men students performing songs predominantly in the style of "barbership harmony" popular in the Victorian era.

glossary. A section in printed material containing a dictionary of special terms and their definitions pertinent to the subject matter.

GMAT. See Graduate Management Admission Test.

goal-directed activity. Activity carried out in order to attain an objective.

government agency education. See employee education.

GPA. See grade-point average.

grade. 1. A mark in the form of a number or letter given usually by a teacher as an evaluation of the academic quality of the student's work in a course, subject, assignment, or examination. See grading system. 2. See grade level.

graded reader. An elementary-school reading textbook designed for use in designated grade levels.

grade-equivalent score. A score on an achievement test earned by one or more schoolchildren that is expressed in such a form as, for example, grade 7, month 1; a form of this kind enables interpreters of the score to see that the score is equivalent in the norms for that test to the average score earned by representative students nationally who are on the level of grade 7, month 1. Also known as grade-level score. Though of easily misinterpreted significance in the recommendations of testing specialists, this type of score is widely used to assess whether children can read (or perform in other subjects) at, above, or below "grade level."

grade inflation. Informal term for practice resulting in a rise in the proportion of higher grades given to students in courses for satisfying less rigorous standards than in preceding years.

grade level. The annual level of instruction and administration to which a child is assigned in schooling in the United States; progression of grade levels and normal ages for those grades in the U.S. are: kindergarten, age 5; grade 1, age 6; grade 2, age 7; grade 3, age 8; and so on, through grade 12, age 17 or 18.

grade-level score. See grade-equivalent score.

grade norm. 1. The average score on a standardized test made by representative students on a given grade level in school; see norms. **2.** The average value of some other characteristic for representative students on a given grade level, such as height or weight.

grade-point average. A value calculated to summarize the relative academic standing of a student (such as rank in class) on the basis of grades received and amounts of work done in courses; usually applied to students in secondary or higher education. It is computed by first converting commonly used course-end letter grades to numerals with a scale normally running A = 4.0, B = 3.0, and so on for C, D, and F. The grade-point value for each course completed by the student is obtained by multiplying the grade-numeral by the point-credit value given the course by the institution (point value in semester-hours, quarter-hours, or Carnegie units). Next the grade-point values for all courses are added. Dividing this sum by the total number of points of study completed yields the grade-point average. Also referred to as GPA, or in informal forms as grade average.

grade retention. In elementary school, requirement for the student's repetition of a grade level through a second school year because of failing academic work; the failure to be promoted to the next grade. Also called held back.

grade school. See elementary education.

grade skipping. Promotion of a student at the end of a school year to start the next school year two grade levels higher instead of only one level higher, because of superior academic performance; as an example, a student promoted from grade 4 to grade 6 would be skipping grade 5.

grading. The process of awarding one or more grades or marks.

grading on the curve. Informal term for the practice of a teacher to award course grades to members of a class or other group not on the basis of fixed standards for passing and higher performance, but on the basis of relative standings within the group; as a result, the distribution of class grades resembles that of a normal distribution curve, with a few students necessarily failing and only a few necessarily getting superior grades. See normal distribution curve.

grading system. 1. System of marks given usually by a teacher as an evaluation of the academic quality of the student's work in a course, subject, assignment, or examination; each educational institution or program adopts its own grading system. Most commonly, institutions in the United States use either a numerical (or percentage) system ranging from 65 (or 70) as the lowest passing mark to a high of 100, or a letter-grade system ranging from "F" for failure through

"A" for excellent. Typical levels of meaning and approximate equivalence in these two predominant systems are as follows:

general meaning	numerical system	letter system
excellent	90–100 (or 95–100)	A (or A-minus to A-plus)
above average	80–90 (or 85–94)	B (or B-minus to A-minus)
average	70–80 (or 75–84)	C (or C-minus to B-plus)
below average	65–70 (or 65–74)	D (or D-minus to C-minus)
failure	below 65	F

2. A pass-fail grading system is one in which students receive course grades consisting only of pass or fail, by individual student request or for all students in a given course or institution. Also called a credit-no-credit grading system. **3.** An alternative grading system used at some experimental colleges and frequently in preschool and early primary education; employs detailed written comments by teachers to provide evaluations of the students' performance instead of letter or numerical grades. Sometimes called informal assessment or summative evaluation. See also grade-point average.

graduate. 1. When pertaining to educational levels, study and teaching beyond the level of the bachelor's degree. A bachelor's degree is normally a prime requirement for admission to graduate study programs. See bachelor's degree. **2.** When pertaining to individuals, persons who have completed requirements of the entire educational program of a school or college; examples of graduation certificates include secondary-school diplomas, college degrees, and graduate-school degrees.

graduate assistant. See assistant.

graduate degree. A second or third degree, either a master's, professional, or doctoral degree, earned in graduate study after the baccalaureate, in a specific discipline or field.

Graduate Management Admissions Test (GMAT). A standardized test almost universally required for admission to graduate business administration studies for the M.B.A. in the United States.

Graduate Record Examinations (GRE). A series of standardized, multiple-choice examinations widely required for admission to graduate study in liberal arts and sciences fields; among the GREs are an aptitude test examining the student in general language and quantitative abilities, and individual advanced tests in each of a number of academic subjects that test the student's knowledge in the area of his or her college major.

graduate school. A school that offers graduate study programs in academic disciplines or professional fields; often a constituent school of a university.

graduation exercises. The formal ceremony at a school or college at the end of a school year, denoting the successful completion of a program or course of study by students, accompanied by the presentation of diplomas or degrees, given by the principal or president, and attended by guest speakers, parents, students, and faculty.

grammar school. Older term referring to an elementary school.

grant. 1. A form of student financial aid; see financial aid. 2. A philanthropic contribution to an institution, for general or specified purposes.

graphic arts. As generally understood, arts related to printing that include typography, lithography, engraving, etching, design, illustration, and drawing.

graying of the campus. A term referring to the marked trend in the 1970s and 1980s for substantially increasing numbers of adult Americans from ages 25 and up to 70 or older to attend higher educational institutions as students. See also lifelong learning.

GRE. See Graduate Record Examinations.

Great Books Program. A complete bachelor's degree program developed in the 1920s and 1930s at the University of Chicago in work led by Robert M. Hutchins and Mortimer Adler; continued today at the St. John's College campuses in Annapolis, MD and Santa Fe, NM. In it, students read classic books selected as the most important works of Western and world civilization from ancient times to the present in such fields as literature, philosophy, the social sciences, and mathematics and the sciences.

grievance procedures. A variety of formal methods used to resolve labor-management conflicts in educational institutions, among which are collective bargaining, arbitration, and ombudsmanship.

group-centered instruction. A nondirective teaching technique in which the teacher acts as a guide in encouraging students toward self-directed learning, high motivation, responsibility, and independence.

group dynamics. Recurrent patterns of interaction occurring between members of small groups, and the study of those patterns and other small-group phenomena in such fields as social psychology and psychotherapy.

group encounter. A psychological technique that features sessions involving a small group of people in which discussions are intimate and direct; used frequently in the 1960s for psychotherapy or personal development.

grouping. 1. The organization and classification of students for instruction based upon certain criteria such as ability, age, or other characteristics. 2. Putting together related words for purposes of better comprehension. 3. Putting together any objects, persons, or ideas for classification and identification.

group standardized test. See individual standardized test.

group therapy. Psychotherapy conducted among a small group of persons by one or more therapists; interaction between the members of the group is thought to have special therapeutic effects for improved personal adjustment or mental health.

growth. The natural life-process development and changes in human development toward the goal of mental, emotional, social, and physical maturity.

growth pattern. A depiction in the form of graphs or data of the growth of a certain type or group of children with respect to one or more characteristics.

growth potential. 1. The limits of the mental, physical, and emotional capacities to which an individual can develop; influenced by heredity and learning. 2. The additional extent to which an individual could develop.

GSL. See Guaranteed Student Loan Program.

Guaranteed Student Loan Program (GSL). Federal and state government program that guarantees and subsidizes interest charges on loans made to students for their postsecondary education costs; represents one of the largest sources of financial aid.

guardian. 1. An adult, in lieu of biological parents, who is legally responsible for the care and upbringing of a child. 2. An adult who is legally responsible for a person unable to care for himself or herself.

guidance. A professional function in education, carried out by qualified guidance counselors as their full-time duties. Includes vocational guidance, concerning development of sound career choices; academic guidance, concerning sound choices of type of program and specific courses; personal guidance, concerning emotional and social adjustment; and college guidance, concerning college planning, admission, and financial aid.

guidance counselor. See guidance.

gymnasium. A room or separate building designed for teaching and practicing physical education, games, and sports such as basketball. May be equipped with locker rooms and showers.

Gymnasium. A classical secondary school in Germany (and other German-speaking nations that include Switzerland and Austria, and also Holland) in which Latin and Greek are emphasized.

H

handicapped child. A child with a moderate to severe physical, mental, or emotional disability that interferes with normal learning. Under federal law such a child has the right to an individually planned program of education. See Education of All Handicapped Children Act.

hand-scoring answer grid. See answer grid.

hands-on. Colloquial term referring to study in which the learner is able to work with the actual equipment, apparatus, or situations involved in practical applications of the subject being taught; for example, hands-on study in the computer field would be provided by sessions of actual experience with computer equipment, while familiar laboratory sessions in science courses represent hands-on learning in scientific subjects.

Hawthorne effect. In an educational experiment, improvement in a result, such as amount learned, due not to any new factor being investigated in the experiment but to motivation stimulated in the subjects by the mere fact of being in an experiment; often observed in a class when any new approach exciting to the students is introduced. Originally observed at a Western Electric Company plant, Hawthorne Works, Chicago, IL, in productivity experiments with lighting; employee productivity was found to go up when light was improved for one group, and then found also to go up when lighting was unchanged for an experimental control group.

Hayes-Binet scale. A test administered to blind children to appraise mental abilities or intelligence.

Head Start Program. A federally funded, locally administered program introduced in 1965 for disadvantaged preschool children from lower-income families. Its purpose was to improve educational performance in later school years by encouraging intellectual, social, and emotional development during ages 3–5. Offered in the program originally were preschool education, hot meals, social workers for family problems, and parent opportunity for community involvement.

headmaster, headmistress. 1. The principal of a private elementary or secondary school. 2. In Europe, used in some cases as the title of a teacher who is the academic and executive head of a school.

health education. An area in school and college curricula in which material about health, health practices, and health attitudes is taught.

health services. 1. Basic medical services offered in a public elementary or secondary school, customarily by a full-time nurse with a consulting physician. In elementary school, physical exams and vision and hearing tests are given routinely, and emergency care is provided when required; in secondary school, the school nurse is available for ordinary complaints, emergencies, and referrals. 2. At some colleges and universities with dormitory students, health services are provided by a diagnostic medical clinic for handling physical and mental problems. Treatment can sometimes be provided in an infirmary or referrals are made. Students pay a fee for their services.

held back. See grade retention.

heterogeneous grouping. Practice of grouping students who represent wide ranges of ability together in the same class, in contrast to homogeneous grouping or tracking.

heuristic method. A teaching technique in which work is arranged so that the learner may make discoveries and connections by himself or herself in order to solve a problem or carry out a task.

hidden curriculum. An implied attitude or stance held by an educational institution whereby it supports and reinforces societal values, such as encouraging good work habits, independence, leadership, achievement, and respect for others.

hierarchy of needs. A theory of human motivation originated by Abraham Maslow, which describes an ascending order of human needs and accomplishments in five successive steps: (1) physiological needs; (2) safety needs; (3) belongingness and love needs; (4) esteem needs; (5) self-actualization. See self-actualization, Maslow, Abraham.

higher education. Education beyond secondary school that is viewed as intellectually more rigorous and sophisticated than that of the secondary level, and that either leads to academic degrees or is on a comparable intellectual level.

Higher Education Act of 1965. Federal statute that provided funds for graduate programs for prospective teachers, including library service improvement, teacher-education improvement, and graduate fellowships for elementary and secondary school teachers. The act also set up the National Teachers Corps to teach in poverty areas.

high-risk student. A student whose background and previous academic performance cause him or her to be perceived as a potential academic failure. A student referred to as "educationally disadvantaged" may prove to be a high-risk student.

high school. A public secondary school in the United States; traditionally, high school includes grades 9 through 12, senior high school includes grades 10 through 12, and junior high school includes grades 7 through 9. Many school districts today have high schools including grades 9–12 and middle schools providing early secondary education in grades 6–8 or 7–8. Some districts have a combined junior-senior high school on one campus. See secondary education.

high school district. A public school district organized for the provision of only secondary education. See school district.

high school equivalency diploma. See equivalency tests, high school equivalency program.

high school equivalency program. Flexible adult basic educational courses and basic developmental activities undertaken by adult learners in preparation for taking the high school equivalency tests, leading to the high school equivalency diploma.

hippie. See counterculture.

history. The study of the past; includes systematic recording and interpretation of past events such as the origins and development of peoples, countries, and institutions. Usually grouped in social sciences.

homebound children. Physically or mentally disabled children who are confined to their homes and who require special home instruction. They are taught by itinerant teachers.

home economics. The study of home management, including knowledge and skills in such areas as nutrition, cooking, sewing, budgeting, and child care; offered in secondary school, and as home economics education at the college and graduate school levels for professional preparation.

homeroom. In secondary schools using departmentalization, a classroom to which a group of students reports each morning; used for purposes of attendance-taking and presenting announcements and administrative information, before the students go to different classrooms for departmentalized instruction. Homeroom is presided over by a homeroom teacher.

home schooling. A substitute for formal schooling in which parents educate their children at home; states differ in their provisions permitting children to receive home schooling.

home study. See correspondence course.

homework. Informal term for teacher assignments and other needed study carried out by the student outside of class hours at home or other locations.

homogeneous grouping. 1. Practice of grouping students who represent a narrow range of ability together in the same class, so that students in a school using the practice are segregated by ability levels; also called tracking. 2. Any similar practice.

honorary degree. An academic title given by a college or university to an individual in recognition of his or her particular merit or accomplishment, without having fulfilled the requirements for an earned academic degree. Honorary degrees are usually doctorates of special kinds.

honorary fraternity, honorary sorority. A society or club usually organized in a professional school of a university for students meeting above-average academic standards; may be related to a professional fraternity. See professional fraternity.

honorary sorority. See honorary fraternity, honorary sorority.

honor roll. A list of student names made public by an educational institution at the end of each marking period, showing those students who have attained a prescribed level of high grades, usually a minimum average of 90 or A in major subjects. At college, also called a Dean's List.

honor society. See honorary fraternity, honor roll, honors study, honor student, National Honor Society, Phi Beta Kappa.

honor study, honors work. Study in one or more courses offered by a college or secondary school that are designated as courses carrying special "honors" distinction and open only to students with high academic ability; such courses are characterized by enriched content, tutorial instruction, and independent study.

honor student. A student who has attained a high academic record that qualifies for honor status as defined by the school or college.

honor system. 1. An organized system at a school or college in which each student is trusted to refrain from unethical acts like cheating or lying, and including a student honor code and some judicial-like means for having students decide punishments for infractions; honor systems are infrequent today. 2. An informal expectation of good behavior, as with trust extended to members of a class that they will not cheat on a test.

hospital nursing school. See nursing school.

hosteling. Educational travel by youth, most often on bicycles, for purposes of learning about a region or foreign country. Done usually during the summer or other school vacation, hosteling is very popular in Europe.

hot lines. Telephone services provided by educational or community personnel, available to students for a range of purposes; hot lines in some cities or towns help with homework, while others aid young people with problems related to drugs, pregnancy, or suicide.

houseperson, houseparents. An adult man, woman, or married couple in residence at a college dormitory or sorority or fraternity house, and having various duties including advising, some chaperoning, and providing friendship.

house plan. 1. The practice by a college of using residence halls called "houses" as centers for certain academic and social activities, as at Harvard College. 2. At some secondary schools and colleges, a method of organizing the institution into two or more constituent divisions called "houses" for instruction and social life, often in order to avoid the impersonality of a large institution.

human capital. Term used in economics to refer to the monetary or financial value represented by the aggregate of productive knowledge and skills in an economic system which result largely from education.

human development. Broadly, the study of the process of normal growth and change of the individual human being that occurs in steps and stages throughout the life cycle.

humanism. 1. A philosophy or outlook espousing the importance of human beings and their welfare. 2. Historically, an intellectual movement during the Renaissance rediscovering the literature, art, and civilization of the ancient Greeks and Romans. See also secular humanism.

humanistic education. An educational approach generally reflecting the outlook of humanism.

humanities, the. 1. As distinct from the sciences and social sciences, academic subjects that include literature, art, music, philosophy, and religion. 2. Historically, the classical languages of Latin and Greek, classical literature and art. See liberal arts.

human relations. An interdisciplinary field of study; treats social interaction between people and groups.

human resources. 1. In management or business administration studies, personnel; as an example, the major study area formerly called personnel administration is now termed management of human resources. 2. Loosely, resource persons. See resource person.

Hutchins, Robert Maynard (1899–). Educator influential in leading innovations in collegiate education and espousing adult learning; he was president and chancellor of the University of Chicago from 1929 to 1951 and, since 1969, has been board chairman of the Center for the Study of Democratic Institutions in Santa Barbara, CA. Among his books are *The Higher Learning in America* (1936), *The Conflict in Education in a Democratic Society* (1953), and *The Learning Society* (1968).

hyperactive child. A child who is excessively active and usually in motion, causing a shortened attention span, possible behavior problems, and learning difficulties in school. Hyperactivity is viewed as one of the major forms of learning disability.

hyperkinetic child. A child who has abnormal and uncontrollable muscular movement, such as spastic tremors. A hyperkinetic child has greater learning difficulties in school than a hyperactive child. See also Ritalin.

hypothesis. A speculative proposition offered to explain a particular phenomenon, or as a premise in reasoning from which a conclusion might be drawn; in order to be validated, a hypothesis needs to be verified by experiments or proven by logic.

I

ideal. A conceptual model or standard of ultimate perfection and excellence.

ideation. Capacity of the mind to think rationally, to imagine, and to deal generally with ideas.

identification. 1. Determination of special characteristics of an object, situation, or condition, so that it may be recognized and distinguished from others. 2. The incorporation of another person's characteristics or feelings into one's own emotional life.

identity crisis. Descriptive term in psychology popularized by Erik Erikson to refer to the need of the adolescent to explore, define, and accept the psychological nature of the "self."

ideography. A system of writing using pictures or symbols instead of letters or words to convey meanings.

ideology. Doctrines or beliefs of a social movement or other large group usually portraying its preferred political or social system.

idiom. 1. In language, a phrase having a figurative meaning defined by common usage that differs from the literal meaning of the words in the phrase. 2. The characteristic pattern or flavor of a language. 3. A word or phrase peculiar to regional speech or specialists' terminology; dialectical vocabulary or jargon.

IE. Industrial engineering, the engineering specialty concerned with the management of industrial production and with the design and analysis of industrial processes.

IEP. See Education of All Handicapped Children Act of 1975.

Ilich, Ivan. See deschooling.

illiteracy. 1. The inability to read and write. 2. Broadly, the state of being ignorant and uneducated.

imagination. The faculty for creating mental constructs of situations, objects, people, or other entities that have not been or are not being perceived or experienced.

imitate. To emulate or copy ideas or behavior deliberately or unconsciously from another.

immaturity. 1. The state of being not yet grown to full adult development. 2. The state of being less advanced in development than other young people of comparable age and background.

immersion program. Informal term for an instructional program in a foreign language in which students spend many consecutive hours a day for a number of days without being allowed to communicate or learn in any language other than the one being studied.

"in absentia". Latin term meaning in his or her absence. For example, during graduation exercises, an announcement may be made to award a degree to a student "in absentia."

inarticulate. 1. Unable to speak comprehensibly or coherently. 2. Occasionally, unable to speak at all.

incentives. External factors that motivate an individual to action, such as the prospect of admission to a leading college as an incentive to serious study.

in-classroom supervision. A method of teacher-evaluation whereby periodic visits are made by a supervisor to a classroom to observe the teacher's instructional work.

independent school. A private school. See private.

independent study. An educational process in which the student is permitted to complete a course of study by learning where and when the student chooses instead of attending regular classes. Independent study by students is guided and evaluated by teachers.

index. In printed material, one or more lists with references indicating where particular information can be found; usually alphabetical in organization.

indirect method. A method of instruction that tends to create situations in which the student is encouraged to learn by active thought rather than by absorbing direct presentations of material to be learned by rote.

individual differences. Wide differences between young individuals of similar ages with respect mainly to mental abilities and other personal qualities that bear on learning; such differences represent a major reason behind methods of individualized instruction.

individual instruction. 1. Teaching an individual exclusively according to his or her needs by such procedures as tutoring or individual conferral. 2. Teaching a class through methods enabling students to learn individually in rate, style, and content; such methods include open education and independent study.

individual standardized test. Psychological test of characteristics such as mental abilities or intelligence, or of personality factors, that is designed to be given individually to the test-taker by a qualified professional. Such a test is standardized through having been given to a valid representative sample of persons. By contrast, a group standardized test is developed for administration to groups of persons at a time. One example of a widely used individual standardized test is the Stanford-Binet Intelligence Scale. See standardized test.

Individualized Education Program. See Education of All Handicapped Children Act of 1975.

individualized instruction. Instruction that is adapted to individual needs within a group, enabling students to proceed individually in rate, style, and even content of their learning. Also called individual instruction. See heterogeneous grouping.

indoctrination. Any attempt to force a particular point of view or set of beliefs on others to the exclusion of differing viewpoints; considered undesirable in the educational systems of democratic nations. See thought control.

inductive reasoning. Logic that draws conclusions by reasoning from the specific to the general; the opposite of deductive reasoning.

industrial arts. General term for the study of a wide range of practical subjects dealing with industry and technology including auto mechanics, cabinet-making, electronics and metal working. Students develop employment skills in working with materials, tools, processes, and products in these subjects.

ineducable. See uneducable child.

ineducable mentally retarded. See mentally retarded.

infant school. 1. Historically, a public preelementary school in the nineteenth century giving instruction in reading and writing to children of ages 4–7, as preparation for elementary school. 2. In England, a school for children of ages 5–7, after which they enter a type of primary school called a junior school.

inference. A logical conclusion drawn from given premises; used systematically in mathematics and philosophy and applied in all fields of thought.

inferiority complex. A constellation of thoughts, feelings, and emotions held by an individual, denoting a self-image of personal or social inadequacy. Originally used by Alfred Adler in psychoanalysis.

inferiority feelings. An emotional attitude reflected in feelings of personal inadequacy that frequently present obstacles to learning.

infirmary. A small health-care unit that offers minimal treatment and hospital services to students and faculty at a college or boarding school.

informal assessment. See grading system.

information explosion. Term used to describe the tremendous acceleration in the output of knowledge starting in the late twentieth century and the resulting consequences for the management of information.

information retrieval. The recovering of designated items of information from large quantities of data stored in a computer.

in-group. Colloquial term for the circle of persons thought to be the most glamorous, successful, and influential in some organization or community.

"in loco parentis". Latin term meaning in place of a parent. Commonly applied to the responsibility of educational institutions for protection and care of their students, especially boarding students.

inner-city school. Contemporary term for a school located in a dilapidated central area of a large city and attended almost entirely by students representing disadvantaged minority groups.

inquiry. A method of seeking knowledge by questioning, observation, and analysis.

in-school suspension. See suspension.

in-service education. Instructional programs to provide for continued professional development of educators during their working years, in contrast to preservice education. In-service programs are usually part-time offerings that carry special professional credits recognized by salary increases. Also called in-service training.

in-service training. See in-service education.

insight. The ability suddenly to grasp or comprehend a central point or solution to a problem by penetrating its real meaning. Popularized originally in Gestalt psychology.

institute. Term used in the names of a variety of schools, colleges, and organizations for research or public service.

institute of technology. Term used in the names of some colleges and universities that concentrate their offerings in the engineering sciences and physical sciences.

institution. 1. General term for an organization providing education, especially an established organization occupying its own buildings and grounds such as an elementary school or university. 2. General term for an organization or facility serving a public purpose, such as a library, museum, hospital, research agency, or prison. 3. A long-established practice, custom, or other feature of the social life of some group, region, or country.

institution of higher learning. See higher education.

institutional school. A school that is part of a larger residential institution such as a prison or a mental hospital.

instruction. 1. A process by which knowledge and skills are developed in learners by teachers or, in some cases, by instructional devices. 2. Any form of teaching.

instructional material. Broad term for any or all of the varieties of printed matter, visual portrayals, audiovisual programs, study specimens, and demonstration or practice apparatus used in education.

instructional media. Types of communications devices or techniques used for teaching purposes, including printed materials as well as newer technical means such as computers, audiovisual aids, and television.

instructional television (ITV). Television programs of lessons that are planned and developed systematically as in a classroom. Generally conducted in universities, and with certain requirements may be given for academic credit.

instructor. 1. Any individual serving in a teaching capacity. 2. In higher education, the lowest rank for a faculty member engaged in teaching at an institution.

instrumental learning. Learning that takes place at a time when it is functional and serves a need, such as learning to speak German before going to visit Germany.

integrate. 1. To make separate parts into a balanced and unified whole. 2. To bring together different subjects into one syllabus. 3. See integration.

integrated program. Term used for an interdisciplinary program of studies. See interdisciplinary.

integration. 1. The objective of the governmental and social movement in the United States to remove the barriers based on racial discrimination that separate blacks and other minorities from the rest of society. Also called desegregation. 2. In education, this object of ending such barriers as substantially realized by actions beginning with the 1954 ruling of the U.S. Supreme Court that all segregation in public schools is "inherently unequal." See "Brown vs. Board of Education of Topeka." 3. Similarly, the ending of segregation for any other minority group in addition to blacks.

intellect. 1. Capacity or power of the mind for thinking and knowing, in contrast to those mental faculties by which the individual feels or wills. 2. Figurative reference to individuals with marked capabilities for thought, or to thinking powers in general.

intelligence. 1. In popular understanding, mental abilities enabling one to think rationally, learn readily, act purposefully, and deal effectively with one's environment. 2. In psychological testing, a term that has been given many different technical meanings concerned with mental abilities such as verbal reasoning, quantitative thinking, abstract analysis and manipulation of geometric shapes, and recognition of similarities and differences between pictured objects. See intelligence test. 3. Information or discoveries, especially when obtained in espionage.

Intelligence Quotient (IQ). Test score made widely popular as an index of relative standing on mental capabilities overall by its early use in the Stanford-Binet Intelligence Scale; IQs originally represented the ratio between a child's "mental age" (a form of total score on the Stanford-Binet or other test) and chronological age. Modern IQ scores of more recent years are no longer ratios, but have been similarly expressed in IQ numbers on a scale in which 100 IQ is the statistical average with some 130 IQ indicating a very high level and 60 IQ a very low level.

intelligence test. Obsolescent term for use as part of the names of standardized tests; tests of the types which had yielded scores in the form of "intelligence quotient" or other measures of intelligence have increasingly been renamed as tests of "mental abilities," "aptitudes," or qualities like scholastic potential. Such long-established individual tests of intelligence as the Wechsler and Stanford-Binet continue to be widely influential in education.

intensive course. A course of study that involves more hours of instruction per day for fewer days of study than a conventional course, in order to insure rapid mastery of the subject matter.

interaction. Reciprocal action and reaction between individuals, groups, or objects, and the resulting influences.

intercollegiate. Pertaining to an athletic game or other contest or activity involving students from different colleges.

intercollegiate sports. See athletic program.

interdisciplinary. Field or project that combines knowledge or experts from traditionally separate subjects or academic disciplines; as examples, physical chemistry is an interdisciplinary subject combining physics and chemistry, while a research study of adolescent drug addiction by a physician, a psychologist, and a sociologist would be an interdisciplinary project.

interest inventory. **1.** An occupational interest inventory, which is a type of psychological test using questions to ascertain a student's pattern of interests; the pattern is compared to patterns typical of persons in various career areas so that a guidance counselor may advise the student about career areas probably congenial to the student. **2.** A similar set of questions about the student's interests designed for counseling use in a connection other than careers, such as social adjustment.

intermediate grades. Usually grades 4, 5, and 6 in elementary school, as differentiated from grades 1, 2, and 3 (primary grades).

intermediate school. Older name for a school that included grades 7 and 8 or 6, 7, and 8; name has been increasingly replaced by middle school in recent years. See middle school.

international educational exchange. Exchange among countries of students, educators, and instructional materials and resources in order to share knowledge and skills and to promote international understanding through education.

international house. A dormitory for foreign students.

International Mathematical Olympiad. International competition in mathematics for secondary-school students held annually; originated among the Communist nations of Eastern Europe in 1959. A United States team has competed since 1974.

International Montessori school. See Montessori method.

international student. See foreign student; also see international educational exchange.

international studies. Interdisciplinary field of study dealing with such subjects as the government, culture, history, and economics of foreign countries, foreign policy, international law, and international relations.

internship. Short-term, supervised work experience in a student's field of interest for which the student may earn academic credit. Work can be part-time or full-time, paid or unpaid, on or off campus.

interscholastic. Pertaining to an athletic game or other contest or activity involving students from different schools.

interscholastic sports. See athletic program.

intersession. In higher education, any period of a few weeks falling between sessions for regular course offerings, such as the January or Mid-Winter Intersession of many colleges today, or the first inter- session before Summer Session. Special short courses may be offered during intersessions.

intramural. Pertaining to an athletic game or other contest or activity involving students at the same school or college.

intramural sports. See athletic program.

intuition. The ability to know something without the use of rational processes, but by spontaneous insight or instinct.

intuitive teaching. In early childhood education, a teaching method in which children engage in direct observation accompanied by dis- cussion of what is observed, and then continue in more observation and discussion.

Iowa tests. Informal term referring to one of two series of achieve- ment tests developed by the late E. F. Lindquist of the University of Iowa and very popular among schools: the Iowa Tests of Educational Development (ITED), for the high-school grades; and the Iowa Tests of Basic Skills (ITBS), for the elementary grades. Each series includes versions for use on various grade levels with subtests in each of several subject areas.

Iowa Tests of Basic Skills (ITBS). See Iowa tests.

Iowa Tests of Educational Development (ITED). See Iowa Tests.

IQ. See Intelligence Quotient.

ITBS. See Iowa tests.

ITED. See Iowa tests.

item. In psychological testing, a question on a standardized test or other type of evaluative instrument.

item bank. A collection of test questions (called "items" by specialists in psychological testing), each coded by objectives, grade level, and content, which may be drawn on to construct tests to meet various requirements; used mainly by publishers of standardized tests.

itinerant teacher. See circuit teacher.

ITV. See instructional television.

Ivy League. Descriptive term of many past years referring to a group of seven of the nation's oldest universities and colleges plus a younger eighth university; the eight are Brown University, Columbia University, Cornell University, Dartmouth College, Harvard University, Princeton University, University of Pennsylvania, and Yale University. Long associated, mainly by tradition, in introducing many features of the modern American university with high academic standards, the colleges in recent decades have joined in a pact to operate the Ivy League as a formal athletic conference officially named the Ivy Group and directed by the Council of Ivy Group Presidents.

J

janitor. See custodian.

J.D. See Doctor of Jurisprudence.

Jesuit college. In higher education, a college or university run by the Society of Jesus, a clerical order of the Roman Catholic church, but often staffed by many lay professors and attended by many non-Catholic students.

Jesuit education. Founded by Ignatius Loyola with the Society of Jesus in the sixteenth century; Jesuit schools became centers of scholarship in the Roman Catholic church with major contributions in the areas of school organization and management.

Jewish Sunday school. Religious instruction in Judaism given to students on Sunday in a temple or synagogue beginning in kindergarten and continuing through secondary school. At age 13, boys and girls usually learn Hebrew in preparation for a bar or bat mitzvah.

job analysis. Term used in vocational guidance meaning the process of determining the features and details of a particular job or the nature of the tasks required within a certain occupational area.

Job Corps program. A national training program, originated under the Economic Opportunity Act of 1964, which provides basic education, job-skill training, and work experience for high school drop-outs between the ages of 16 and 22.

junior. 1. A student in the 11th grade of secondary school or in the third year of a four-year college program. **2.** Informal term describing a rank lower than a senior one. **3.** Occasionally, a term describing a young person.

junior college. See two-year college.

junior high school. Older term for a secondary school providing instruction on levels just prior to those of a senior high school, and sometimes operated as part of a junior-senior high school occupying a single campus; grade levels of instruction were originally 7, 8, and 9, but among schools today may be 7 and 8, or 8 and 9. See middle school.

junior prom. See prom.

junior-senior high school. A secondary school providing education usually in grades 7 through 12. Students in the lower grades through 8 are usually in a building separate from students in the higher grades.

junior varsity. See varsity.

junior year abroad (JYA). A practice at some colleges and universities whereby a junior-year American student spends the year abroad studying at a foreign university for academic credit.

juvenile delinquent. Generally, a youth under the age of 18 who commits an antisocial or criminal act and who may be suspended from school. A juvenile delinquent usually receives mitigated punishment before the law.

JYA. See junior year abroad.

K

K. Customary abbreviation for kindergarten, as in grades K–3 (grades kindergarten through three).

Kerr, Clark (1911–). Higher education leader; after having served as professor of industrial relations at the University of California at Berkeley from 1945 to 1952, he was appointed chancellor of the institution. He became president of the overall University of California system in 1958 and continued in that post until appointed director of the Carnegie Commission on Higher Education in 1967. Sponsored by the foundation, the Carnegie Corporation of New York, the Commission carried out numerous book-length studies of the future of higher education.

kindergarten. A school-year grade in elementary schools for the instruction of five-year-olds, usually attending half-day sessions; characterized by play activities having educational and social value, with emphasis on preparation for reading and writing in grade 1 in the next school year. See Friedrich W. A. Froebel.

knowledge. 1. The aggregate of facts, information, and principles that an individual has acquired through learning and experience; formal education seeks to raise levels of knowledge systematically. 2. The body of such material acquired by humankind, or some portion of it.

L

laboratory. 1. Physical facilities designed and equipped for carrying out scientific experiments in student practice, teaching, or research. 2. Facilities equipped to serve as another kind of workplace, as with a room called the reading skills development laboratory.

laboratory school. A school conducted to introduce or demonstrate educational experiments. See also demonstration school.

labor-relations study programs. Course offerings and degree majors at some colleges and universities concerning study and research in the broad field of labor-management relations.

labor union education. Educational programs offered by labor unions for their members; extensive and diverse coursework is provided in some of these programs.

land-grant institutions. State universities or colleges originally founded with grants of land from the federal government made under the Morrill Act of 1862; totaling some 70 institutions, they include a number of the largest state universities in the United States, and almost all of the country's universities that have colleges of agriculture.

language arts. 1. Verbal skills used in communication. 2. Term used chiefly in elementary education to refer to a group of subjects taught to develop English-language skills such as reading, spelling, English composition, and speech.

language laboratory. Room or rooms especially equipped for foreign-language learning and individual practice and development by students; equipment normally includes audio tapes and headphones, and may provide for individualized instruction by a teacher as well as independent practice.

latchkey child. A child who carries the door key to his or her home and who, after the school day, returns to a home from which parents are absent because of employment.

late bloomer. Informal term for a student who achieves at higher academic levels later in his or her education than appeared likely at earlier stages.

latent achiever. A student whose academic performance lags behind the expectations of his or her potential as indicated by occasional signs or aptitude measurement. Also referred to as a "late bloomer."

latent learning. Term used to describe learning that occurs without being evidenced in the student's performance when it is acquired, but which later becomes evident when occasion to demonstrate it arises.

law enforcement. The field of study offering instruction concerned with the work of police officers and with police administration; also called criminal justice or police science. See criminology.

law school. A graduate school, usually affiliated with a university, where study is required in order to become a lawyer or attorney in the United States; professional educational programs normally take three years of full-time study to complete and lead to the J.D. degree.

Law School Admission Test (LSAT). A standardized, multiple-choice examination almost universally required for admission to law schools in the United States; it is sponsored by the Law School Admission Council and administered by Educational Testing Service.

lay reader. A person other than a professional teacher who is skilled in English and who assists an English teacher by reading and marking student compositions.

lay teacher. A teacher in a school sponsored by a religious body who is not a member of the clergy or of a religious order like those for monks or nuns.

leadership style. Used generally to describe the style of management of an administrator; among most common broad categories of such styles are authoritarian, democratic, laissez-faire.

league. See athletic conference.

learning. 1. The process of acquiring knowledge, skills, and beliefs through study, education, and experience. 2. Knowledge, especially that developed by scholarly research.

learning capacity. The receptivity of an individual to learning, and the maximum amount of information and knowledge that the individual is able to learn, retain, assimilate, and apply.

learning center. 1. Specific area set aside within a classroom by the teacher; in it, various materials are provided for one or more students to examine, explore, and manipulate without direct teacher instruction. 2. Term variously applied to facilities providing study materials, and sometimes special instruction. See also learning resources center.

learning curve. Graphed line showing the rate at which a student group typically learns new material in a course or subject; learning curves usually show the most rapid rises in amount of learning in the opening hours or days of a course, and continued high levels in amount of material learned later in the course.

learning disability. A disorder in one or more of the processes required in using and understanding written or spoken material. The disorder may be evident in compromised ability to speak, think, read, write, spell, listen, or do mathematical operations. Such disorders usually include conditions of brain injury, brain dysfunction, dyslexia, perceptual difficulties, and aphasia. Normally not included are learning problems representative of traditional special education categories: blind (or partially sighted), deaf, physically disabled, mentally retarded, and emotionally disturbed. See special education.

learning modalities. Pertaining to a physical sense like sight that the individual uses most as learning takes place; the prime modalities are visual, aural, and tactile.

learning objective. See behavioral objectives.

learning plateau. A period or stage when the rate at which a student or group has been increasing in amount learned levels off either as normally observed by teachers or for special reasons. See learning curve.

learning resources center. An adjunct library facility at a school or college that provides a variety of equipment and materials for individual study, including audiovisual aids, and devices and materials to help improve reading and learning skills.

learning society. See lifelong learning.

learning style. The way in which a student is best able to learn: visually, aurally, by motor activity, or a combination of these.

learning theory. A theory developed to explain the ways in which individuals learn, in general, or in special areas; most often associated with a particular psychologist, psychological school, or educator.

leave of absence. An authorized absence of an educator from a full-time position for a specific length of time, usually a term or year. See sabbatical leave. Occasionally, a similar authorized absence for a student.

lecture method. A method of teaching in which the subject matter is presented orally to a class with a minimal amount of student participation.

lecturer. Title given to persons engaged under a wide variety of arrangements to teach at a college or university; usually used as "lecturer in (subject)," the title tends to signify part-time, temporary teaching status.

lesson. 1. A student assignment made by the teacher; the day's homework in a subject. 2. Material presented to a class by the teacher in an instructional period; the day's teaching in a subject for a class. 3. Unit of a course, especially one taught by correspondence instruction. 4. Conclusion drawn on the basis of experience or study.

lesson plan. A teacher's outline of significant points to be covered in a class session and, in addition, including learning objectives, methods, and materials to be used, assignments, and evaluation steps.

letter. Usually the first letter of the substantive name of a school or college given to a student for qualifying as a member of a varsity team; the letter is worn on a school sweater or jacket.

letter grading system. See grading system.

letters. 1. A synonym for literature and literary arts. 2. In higher education, older synonym for the arts, as a faculty of letters instead of a faculty of arts.

liberal arts. A term with various complex meanings that all refer to study of the academic subjects which make up the humanities (including languages, literature, philosophy, fine arts); the social sciences (such as economics, sociology, anthropology, history, political science); and the sciences (biology, chemistry, and physics, and including mathematics). Also called liberal arts and sciences, and arts and sciences.

liberal arts and sciences. See liberal arts.

library network. Association of two or more libraries for the purpose of providing better services at lower costs, in part by making the holdings of every library available to users of any member library.

library school. A graduate school or division in higher education for the preparation of students in professional librarianship; offers a study program normally taking two years of full-time study to complete and leading to the master's degree in library science.

library science. The study of the professional administration of libraries and their resources, including the methods of acquisition, organization, and utilization of information.

Licensed Practical Nurse (LPN). A person who satisfactorily completes state licensing requirements after graduating from a one-year or two-year LPN program offered in hospitals, community colleges, and adult education. The LPN typically provides most of the patient's basic hospital care.

licensing. See certification.

life-adjustment course. A type of course in wholesome psychological adjustment and personal health that was popular in high schools in the United States in the 1920s and 1930s but that has since virtually vanished.

life-experience credit. Term loosely and often mistakenly applied to degree credit awarded by colleges to adults for prior college-level learning acquired outside college classrooms. See also experiential learning.

lifelong learning. Process by which an individual acquires formal and informal education continually throughout adulthood for necessary career development and valuable personal enrichment; increasingly prevalent in the United States and other industrialized nations from the 1970s on, in part as a result of a lifelong learning movement led by government officials and college educators (a movement to help Americans develop into what some educators termed "a learning society").

linguistics. The study of the nature, structure, and development of languages.

literature search. An extensive exploration of a given topic in library research.

little red schoolhouse. Figurative term often used with nostalgia to refer to the one-room schoolhouses in rural settings (and frequently painted red) that typified much of elementary schooling in America in the nineteenth century and well into the twentieth century.

LL.B. See Doctor of Jurisprudence.

load. See student load, teacher load, teaching load.

loan. See Guaranteed Student Loan Program, National Direct Student Loan, financial aid.

local autonomy. A principle under which local school districts are left free by state governments to make their own decisions regarding the administration of their schools. Also referred to as autonomy of the school district.

logic. 1. The scientific study of the general principles of inference and proof, or reasoning. 2. The abstract structure of an argument or a body of knowledge.

lower division. Pertaining to college studies on the level of the freshman and sophomore years, as distinguished from upper division pertaining to the level of the last two college years.

loyalty oath. An oath of allegiance that has been required in some instances for school employment; has used various criteria of loyalty, usually the support of the country and the United States Constitution.

LPN. See Licensed Practical Nurse.

LSAT. See Law School Admission Test.

M

M. Abbreviation for "Master of" when used as the initial letter in abbreviations for various types of master's degrees, as in M.A. and M.B.A. See master's degree.

machine scoring. The scoring of test questions by special computer equipment that reads answers electrically or optically, used on a very large scale for the most popular series of standardized, multiple-choice tests, and generally feasible only for multiple-choice or true-false tests having separate answer sheets.

machine shop. In secondary school or technical postsecondary education, the physical facilities with metal-working machines where students learn the skills of the trade of machinist; also informally used to refer to industrial arts courses teaching those skills.

magna cum laude. See cum laude.

magnet school. Figurative term given currency in connection with desegregation; refers to a public school funded to have extremely attractive programs that will draw an essentially integrated enrollment from a specially enlarged or districtwide attendance zone.

mainstream. The practice of assigning any child who is unusually low or high in learning capabilities to attend regular classes with the wide range of normal children. See Education for All Handicapped Children Act of 1975.

major. The subject (or interdisciplinary combination of subjects) in which a candidate for a bachelor's degree (or graduate degree) concentrates studies in the last year or two of full-time degree work; formally termed subject or field of major concentration, in statements of degree requirements.

makeup class. 1. A class conducted by a teacher to provide additional teaching time and help in work already covered in regular class. 2. Additional class time scheduled to cover classwork not yet taught because of regular class cancellation.

maladjustment. Some degree of lack of smooth adaptation on the part of the individual to surrounding conditions, especially to other people.

management. In higher education, the broad field of instruction and study concerned with management or work as an executive in business or government organizations; see business administration.

management by objectives (MBO). Management technique centered on defining formal goals and attaining them with frequent planning and evaluation; a business approach applied in educational administration.

management development education. 1. Instructional programs offered by corporations and government agencies to develop the capabilities of their management personnel; includes courses taken in groups or in individual study. 2. Similar instructional programs of short courses offered by graduate business schools.

Mann, Horace (1796-1859). Attorney, American educator, first secretary of the Massachusetts state board of education from 1837 to 1848, widely regarded as the leading figure in the public school movement in the crucial early years from the 1830s through the 1850s; in 1852 became the first president of Antioch College and pioneered there by demonstrating the practicality of coeducation and of college education for blacks.

Manpower Development and Training Act. A federal law enacted by Congress in 1962 to enable states, with aid from the federal government, to help areas counter the problem of unemployment. Federal aid was available in four ways: (1) low-interest, long-term loans to help business enterprises expand; (2) loans to communities to provide public facilities for existing firms; (3) technical assistance for communities for implementing programs of economic development; and (4) programs to retrain workers in new skills, and providing workers with minimal financial aid while in training. The effort was largely administered by the Secretary of Labor, and the Secretary of Health, Education and Welfare coordinated the training programs. Incorporated into CETA in 1973. See Comprehensive Education and Training Act.

manual. 1. Publication accompanying a textbook and presenting such content as related material, answers to exercises, additional exercises, and reading lists; issued in the form of teachers' manuals, and of student manuals. 2. A publication presenting explanatory material or technical data.

marine biology. See oceanography.

mark. 1. Evaluation given by the teacher of the quality of performance shown by the student on an assignment or examination, with the evaluation usually stated in the form of a numerical grade or letter grade; see grading system. 2. Student's score on a test. 3. The act of assigning such evaluations.

marketing. The field of study in business curricula in secondary and higher education concerned with merchandising and sales; a major in bachelor's and master's degree programs in business administration.

marking system. See grading system.

mascot. An animal or other figure often wearing school colors, which is supposed to bring good luck to a college or school team in competitive events. Among such sports mascots are a bulldog for Yale, a tiger for Princeton, and a lion for Columbia.

Maslow, Abraham (1908–1970). American psychologist best known for his contribution to motivation theory in *Motivation and Personality* (1954), and *Towards a Psychology of Being* (1962). See also hierarchy of needs, self-actualization.

mass education. 1. Loose term referring to special endeavors by mass media including the press and broadcasting that seek to bring significant cultural or informational material before large audiences. 2. Informal term for universal public education provided free of charge.

Master of Business Administration (M.B.A.). Master's degree awarded on graduation from a graduate school of business at a university, and usually requiring completion of a two-year, full-time study program or its equivalent.

Master of Education (M.Ed.). A degree awarded the individual for study beyond the bachelor's degree in professional teacher education, and roughly comparable to the M.A. or M.S. degree in education; usually requires a year of full-time study to earn.

Master of Social Work (M.S.W.). The professional degree in the field of social work, normally earned in two years of full-time graduate study or its equivalent.

master's degree. The first degree on the graduate level, beyond the bachelor's degree, in many fields; normally earned in one year or two years of full-time study (or equivalent amounts of part-time study), depending on the field and the institution. See bachelor's degree.

master's thesis. A research paper often required for the master's degree in an academic field, in addition to full-time coursework on the master's level.

mastery learning. An approach to education or instruction in which the learning objectives that students should attain in a course or subject are held constant, but in which the time allowed for attaining those objectives is permitted to vary from student to student; all students are thus enabled to achieve mastery learning of that body of knowledge. The concept of mastery learning was made widely familiar for several decades starting in the 1950s especially through the work of Benjamin Bloom, professor of education at the University of Chicago.

matching grants program. In educational philanthropy, any program in which a potential donor offers to contribute sums to match the monetary gifts of other benefactors to an institution; the matching grants may equal or be some multiple or fraction of the gifts of other benefactors. Alumni matching grants programs represent the most widespread type of such programs; in them, large employers match the gifts made by their employees to the colleges from which the employees graduated.

matching test question. A form of examination question in which the student is asked to match the items listed in two or more columns, such as rulers of countries named in one column with the nations they headed listed in a second column.

material, materials. See instructional material.

mathematics. 1. The science of quantities or numbers, including the relationships between them and geometric forms. 2. Applications of this science in other academic disciplines or in practical fields such as consumer mathematics or business arithmetic.

mathematical score. See Scholastic Aptitude Test.

matriculate. The act of securing institutional approval to be enrolled in a college or university as a candidate taking course credits toward a specific academic degree. Students who take courses without having those credits count toward a degree are nonmatriculated students.

maturation. The process of growing or unfolding to a fully developed state or adulthood.

maturity. The stage at which an organism has reached full development or completion of the process of growth; figuratively, also applied to phenomena.

M.B.A. See Master of Business Administration.

MCAT. See Medical College Admission Test.

M.D. See Doctor of Medicine.

ME. Mechanical engineering, the engineering specialty concerned primarily with machinery and its design, and with industrial production equipment.

mean. See average.

measure of central tendency. See central tendency.

measurement. 1. The process of ascertaining the quantitative extent of a given physical characteristic with the use of an appropriate scale and measuring device. 2. A quantity ascertained by this process. 3. In education, term for the use of standardized tests or other psychological testing devices to appraise abilities, achievement, or other characteristics of individuals; also applied to the use of such tests in evaluating educational processes.

M.Ed. See Master of Education degree.

median. See average.

media studies. Informal term referring to study or coursework concerned with such communications media as the press and broadcasting.

mediated teaching. Term sometimes used for teaching that is presented to learners via one of the communications media such as film or television rather than face-to-face.

Medical College Admission Test (MCAT). A standardized, multiple-choice test almost universally required for admission to medical schools in the United States.

medical school. Informal term for a graduate school in the United States awarding the Doctor of Medicine (M.D.) degree that represents the main requirement for becoming licensed to practice as a physician; normally, the bachelor's degree is required for admission to medical school, and medical students spend four years of full-time study earning the M.D. degree.

memory span. The degree to which the number of items can be recalled correctly after one presentation or hearing of the material.

MENSA. An international organization for adult individuals with exceptionally high intelligence quotients (IQs).

mental ability. A relatively general type of capability of thought processes evaluated by the kind of standardized test that is often called a test of mental abilities; among such abilities are verbal ability, numerical ability, and spatial visualization ability.

mental age. Theoretical concept for the level of intelligence developed by a child expressed as an age at which average children exhibit that level of intelligence; for example, a mental age of 10 years would mean the child has an intelligence level corresponding to that of average 10-year-olds. Introduced with the concept of intelligence quotient, and now obsolescent in education. See intelligence quotient.

mental health. The state of wholesomeness and well-being of the mind, including the emotional balance necessary for successful personality adjustment and normal social functioning.

mental measurement. Obsolescent term for the use of standardized tests or other psychological testing devices to appraise intellectual capabilities or personality characteristics. See measurement.

Mental Measurements Yearbook (MMY). An extensive standard reference on psychological tests that was originated and edited for many years by Oscar Buros.

mental retardation. See mentally retarded.

mental set. A state of emotional and mental readiness, receptivity, and motivation to engage in a particular learning activity. Without the proper mental set, learning is made more difficult.

mentally retarded. A handicapping condition evidenced by slower than normal general development, seriously below-average learning capacities, and immature social adjustment, usually evidenced from an early age; such individuals need schooling that uses techniques of special education. Educable mentally retarded children are ones judged to have the capacity to lead normal adult lives if properly educated; ineducable mentally retarded children are ones judged to be below the educable levels of functioning.

mentor. 1. In higher education, an instructor or supervisor responsible for guiding a student through a course of study in nontraditional education such as a college degree program. 2. Any teacher or counselor who is highly respected and revered by students.

merit scholarship. 1. An award in the National Merit Scholarship Program; see National Merit Scholarship Program. 2. A scholarship offered by a college for students it considers to be of unusually high academic ability, and often a scholarship awarded without regard to the winner's financial need. See no-need scholarship.

methods courses. Required courses during teacher training in how to teach a specific subject, or standard classroom procedures that may apply to teaching any subject.

merit system. In public school teaching, a plan through which teachers would advance in salary and position in the school system according to demonstrated capabilities rather than only by seniority and formal credentials.

metallurgy. The engineering science concerned with metals.

metaphysics. One of the major traditional branches of philosophy, originated by Aristotle; includes ontology (analysis of the nature of existence) and cosmology (analysis of the nature of the cosmos or universe), and also involves epistemology (analysis of the nature of knowledge).

metapsychology. Speculative psychology; psychological analysis treating matters beyond experimental or empirical investigation.

meteorology. The branch of the earth sciences concerned with the atmosphere.

methodology. The set of systematic procedures and practices employed in a process or discipline or some part of that set.

M.F.A. Master of Fine Arts degree; see master's degree.

microfiche. A small sheet of microfilm on which multiple pages of books or other documents are shown; a microreader machine is used to magnify the reduced text.

microfilm. A film on which reduced-size images of documents are reproduced; may be read only through special magnifying viewers. Microfilm copies of many periodical issues and other printed works are found in school and public libraries and are valued as space-savers.

middle school. 1. A school providing instruction on the level of early secondary education for grades 6, 7, and 8, or 7 and 8. See junior high school. 2. A school providing instruction on any consecutive grade levels between early elementary grades and secondary grades.

midterms, midyears. Informal terms referring to examinations given in the middle of the academic term or year, as with "finals" for final examinations at year-end or course-end.

migrant child. Child of migrant farm workers who usually live at the edge of poverty and move to different areas and school districts for employment every few weeks; such a child often presents special difficulties to public schools due to his or her transient state and deprived cultural background.

military school. 1. Popular term applied to a private school for boys at which the students wear military uniforms, belong to a school cadet corps in which each student holds a military rank, and engage in formal military drill and other military practices. 2. Broadly, any educational institution that conducts instruction primarily in subjects concerned with warfare and the armed forces conducting it.

minicourse. An abbreviated course with limited objectives, requiring less than normal course time; taken frequently by teachers and adult students.

minimum competency testing. See competency test.

minischool. A small school affiliated with a larger school that uses methods of alternative education for pupils with special needs or problems. See also alternative schools.

minor. 1. A person under the legal age for full civil rights, traditionally 21 or 18 in a number of states. 2. For a bachelor's or graduate degree candidate, a field in which the student concentrates degree studies as with a major but to a lesser extent. See major.

minority group. A social group of persons whose race, religion, or ethnic background differs from the race, religion, or ethnic background of the majority of persons in their country; major minority groups in the United States include black Americans, Asian Americans, Hispanic Americans, and Native Americans.

MLA. See Modern Language Association.

misconduct. Action on the part of a student, teacher, or administrator that violates a rule of upright behavior that is either stated or clearly understood in an educational institution.

mission school. A school conducted by missionaries of a religious organization as part of its efforts to win converts and spread its religious views.

MMY. See Mental Measurements Yearbook.

mnemonic device. A technique or type of apparatus used to aid memorization, as with a rhyming jingle or flash cards.

mobile classroom. A trailer, van, or other vehicle outfitted as a classroom that can be moved wherever needed for instruction.

mock exam. Simulation of an examination that students will take at a future date; given by teachers to provide practice and familiarization with material for students.

modal age. The age or span of ages in years and months that is thought to typify most closely young people on a particular grade level in schooling, like grade 3 or grade 7.

mode. See average.

modeling. 1. In education, figurative term for a form of observational learning by imitation of a person taken as a model by the learner. See observational learning. 2. In the fine arts, shaping or molding a solid substance into a sculptural art work.

model school. See demonstration school.

Modern Language Association. A professional organization of secondary and higher education teachers of English and modern foreign languages.

modern languages. Foreign languages as currently used, as distinguished from the major ancient or classical languages, Latin and Greek.

module. 1. A period of time in a daily school schedule. 2. A unit of study in a course or other learning program. 3. Any other type of segment in an organized entity, such as a repeated element in an architectural design.

monitor. 1. A student appointed by the teacher or the school administration to assist with a school task, such as directing traffic or erasing blackboards. 2. A device that makes continuous observations of some situation or process, as with closed-circuit TV apparatus serving as a monitor on a building entrance. 3. To observe continuously and possibly regulate a process or endeavor.

monograph. A comprehensive treatment of a topic by a scholarly author that is often shorter than customary book length.

Montessori, Maria (1870–1952). Italian physician and educator. See Montessori method.

Montessori method. A system of schooling from preschool years on developed by Dr. Maria Montessori and adopted in numerous schools around the world; now most widely used in small Montessori schools operated for preschool children that feature use of special Montessori physical materials for teaching letters, numbers, and other abstractions, and of independently pursued learning activities for each child under a special technique of Montessori guidance by the teacher. Montessori schools tend to be of two types: "International Montessori," which adhere rigidly to the original techniques and materials of Dr. Montessori; and "American Montessori," which apply what proponents view as the Montessori method modernized to make it broader, more effective, and up-to-date. See Montessori, Maria.

moot court. Simulation of a courtroom environment in a classroom in which students role-play lawyers, judges, plaintiffs, and defendants. May be used as a learning technique in law school, debate practice, social studies, or political science.

Moral Majority. The group for political action founded and led by the fundamentalist minister, The Rev. Jerry Falwell, who conducts the widely televised broadcast ministry, "Old Time Gospel Hour," and is pastor of Thomas Road Baptist Church in Lynchburg, VA; in education, the group espouses conservative practices.

Morrill Acts. The Morrill Act of 1862 (which provided for land grants to the states for use in establishing colleges especially to teach agriculture, mechanical arts, and military science); and the Morrill Act of 1890 (which authorized annual appropriations to these colleges). See land-grant colleges and universities.

mortarboard. A traditional type of academic hat worn as part of academic dress by educators and students at graduation exercises and other ceremonies; consists of a close-fitting kind of skullcap with a large, flat square piece attached on top and with a tassel affixed to the center of the square. The mortarboard is commonly black in color and worn with an academic robe of the same color; the mortar-board and the robe are the "cap and gown" of academic dress.

motif. In art or musical composition, a theme. See theme.

motivation. See achievement motivation.

motor-activity principle. A fundamental principle of the kindergarten as conceived by Friedrich Froebel and growing out of theories that young children learn primarily through motor or physical activities such as building, drawing, modeling, running, and singing. See Friedrich W. A. Froebel.

motor development. Growth in physical coordination or skills of physical movement during infancy especially, concerning such functions as posture, locomotion, and hand-arm-eye movements in manipulation.

M.S.W. See Master of Social Work.

multihandicapped. Pertains to an individual with two or more serious mental or physical dysfunctions.

multilingual. Having fluency in each of several languages.

multiple-choice test. A type of test in which one answers the questions by selecting the correct or most appropriate choice from among several answers that are presented with each question; answers are usually marked by the examinee on a separate answer sheet provided with the test. Most standardized tests used in education are of the multiple-choice type. See distractor.

multiplication facts. See number facts.

multiplication tables. See number facts.

municipal college. A college sponsored by a municipal government, as with Los Angeles City College.

municipal control. Term referring to a degree of control over the school system in a city by authorities of the municipal government, through such devices as powers to appoint board of education members or to determine revenues for operating the school system.

music. 1. Vocal or instrumental sound in patterns having rhythm, melody, or harmony. 2. The art or science of organizing sounds in succession to form aesthetically satisfying or theoretically coherent compositions. 3. Notations, performances, or types of compositions of such organized sounds.

music appreciation. See appreciation course.

music education. The field of study concerned with preparing individuals for careers in the teaching of music.

musicology. The nontechnical study of the development of music as analyzed within the contexts of history, science, and philosophy.

N

NAEP. See National Assessment of Educational Progress.

NAIA. See National Association of Intercollegiate Athletics.

named professorship. See chair.

National Achievement Scholarship Program. Annual program offering many college scholarships for outstanding black students on a national, competitive basis; operated as part of the National Merit Scholarship Program. See National Merit Scholarship Program.

National Assessment of Educational Progress (NAEP). Agency that assesses with its own tests the comparative levels of accomplishment of young people nationally in such subject areas as reading, mathematics, science, and composition (or writing skills), at intervals of several years; children aged 9, 13, and 17 are evaluated in its program, which is authorized by the United States Congress, financed by the National Institute of Education, and conducted by the Education Commission of the States, based in Denver, CO.

National Association of Intercollegiate Athletics (NAIA). An organization regulating intercollegiate athletics nationwide in the United States.

National Center for Education Statistics (NCES). The branch of the federal government responsible for collecting and reporting on data concerning education in the United States and other nations.

National Collegiate Athletic Association (NCAA). The largest organization regulating intercollegiate athletics in the United States.

National Congress of Parents and Teachers. See Parent-Teacher Association.

National Direct Student Loan (NDSL). Type of student loan that was provided through federal subsidy at especially favorable terms including interest during repayment after graduation as low as 3% annually; NDSL loans were made available under programs authorized by the United States Congress starting in 1958 and continuing through 1981, and are for students in postsecondary education.

National Education Association (NEA). A major professional association of teachers and other educators in the United States, with several million members; organized with chapters in individual public school systems that serve as collective bargaining agents.

National Endowment for the Arts. Agency of the federal government funded by Congressional appropriation to make grants for projects in the arts.

National Endowment for the Humanities. Agency of the federal government funded by Congressional appropriation to make grants for projects in the humanities.

National Home Study Council (NHSC). Association with national recognition for accrediting institutions offering correspondence study. See correspondence course.

National Honor Society. A student society with chapters at secondary schools throughout the United States; students become members by attaining specified high levels of academic achievement.

National Institute of Education (NIE). Agency within the United States Department of Education concerned with educational research and development.

National Merit Scholarship Program. A widely publicized annual program introduced in the 1950s awarding college scholarships to students selected for especially high academic ability; the first step in its annual selection process comes every fall when tenth-grade students take the initial selection test, the "Preliminary Scholastic Aptitude Test-National Merit Scholarship Qualifying Test" (PSAT-NMSQT) of The College Board. See Preliminary Scholastic Aptitude Test-National Merit Scholarship Qualifying Test; National Achievement Scholarship Program.

National Science Foundation (NSF). An independent agency in the executive branch of the federal government that supports basic research and education in science largely through grants to nonprofit institutions and fellowships to individuals.

natural science. One of the physical sciences or life sciences dealing with phenomena in nature, such as genetics, as distinct from the fields of the social sciences or the humanities.

nature-nurture controversy. A controversial question in education that seeks to evaluate the relative importance of hereditary factors versus environmental influences in determining individual behavior.

NCAA. See National Collegiate Athletic Association.

NCES. See National Center for Education Statistics.

NDSL. See National Direct Student Loan.

NEA. See National Education Association.

need. See achievement need, financial need.

need analysis. In student financial aid for college, an extensive procedure for estimating as justly as possible the annual amount the student (and the student's family) can reasonably afford to spend for college expenses. See financial aid, financial need.

negative reinforcement. In the learning theories of B. F. Skinner and other behavioral psychologies that underlie programmed instruction, punishment for giving a wrong answer to a question posed after a unit of reinforcement. See programmed instruction.

negative transfer. See transfer of learning.

negativism. A kind of behavior encountered in some children that is marked by sustained opposition to action requested by one or more older persons.

neighborhood school. A public school that draws all or almost all of its students from its surrounding locale, which is defined by the school system as that school's attendance zone. See school attendance zone.

neighborhood youth corps. A work and counseling program for youths from low-income families that was set up by the United States Department of Labor for the Office of Economic Opportunity in the 1960s.

Network for Learning. A continuing education program for adults, offered on a profit-making basis originally in New York City and providing a wide variety of four-week classes and one-day seminars in such areas as business, theater, sports, and health; courses are taught in such environments as corporate boardrooms, theaters, and private residences. No academic credit, degrees, or vocational training are offered.

neurolinguistics. The study of the biological foundations of language involving the parts of the brain associated with language acquisition and use.

neurosis. A type of psychological difficulty, often with an obscure cause, which is evidenced by depression, anxiety, phobias, obsessions, or other psychological malfunctioning, but is not severe enough to warrant treatment by hospitalization.

new math, new mathematics. A type of curriculum in arithmetic and mathematics through elementary and secondary schooling that was widely introduced starting in the 1950s at the urging of professional organizations of mathematicians and mathematics teachers; it represented what was viewed as a more unified system of teaching mathematics through use of the mathematical theory of sets and other basic mathematical concepts.

NHSC. See National Home Study Council.

NIE. See National Institute of Education.

noncredit. Refers to courses or other instructional offerings in postsecondary institutions that do not carry credits applicable toward college degrees, but are taken by students for their career value or cultural interest. See continuing education units, credits.

noncredit course. A course of study that offers no academic credits toward a degree. Such courses are widely given in continuing education and adult education.

nondenominational. See nonsectarian.

no-need scholarship. Informal term applied to a scholarship for student financial aid that is provided without any consideration of the financial need of potential recipients, and without application of the widespread college practice of adjusting the amount of a scholarship award to fit the winner's financial need. In some cases, also called a merit scholarship. See financial need, merit scholarship.

nongraded class. A class grouping of students who are similar in academic achievement but dissimilar in chronological age; used in somewhat innovative approaches to schooling, like open education. Also termed ungraded class, family grouping.

nonmatriculated. See matriculate.

nonresident. 1. In the case of a public college or university, pertains to students who are not residents of the state, county, or city sponsoring the college; students who are residents as officially defined by the college usually are subject to substantially lower tuition and fee charges and to less demanding admissions standards than is the case for nonresident students. 2. In the case of a public school system, pertains to any student who has some valid reason for attending school in the system but whose legal residence is not within the school district.

nonsectarian. 1. Not reflecting the views of some religious group. 2. Not affiliated with a religious group.

nonselective admissions. An alternate term for an open admissions policy of a college or school. See open admissions, selective admissions.

nontraditional study. Term applied to innovative programs in post-secondary education that provide greater access to educational opportunities for adult learners; given wide currency in this sense during the 1960s by the Commission on Nontraditional Study of The College Board.

nonverbal communication. Communication between persons without use of words.

nonverbal test questions. Questions in standardized tests of general mental abilities (often called intelligence tests in previous decades) that are geometric or pictorial in nature, and for which directions in words are kept as simple as possible; such questions are used to help make the test valid for children who are bright but possibly limited in their verbal facility in Standard English.

norm. 1. Generally, a standard for guiding sound judgment or proper behavior. 2. See norms.

normal. 1. With respect to people, typical and not characterized by any pronounced extreme in personal qualities nor by any serious physical or psychological difficulties. 2. With respect to measurements of some quality, distributed in accordance with the normal distribution curve. See normal distribution curve.

normal child. A child thought to stand within the middle half or two-thirds of the curves of normal distribution with respect to such measurable characteristics as growth, physical size and capabilities, mental abilities, achievement in school subjects, and emotional stability and maturity.

normal distribution curve. In statistics, a graphed line taking the form of a bell-shaped curve that represents a theoretically normal distribution of any factor varying purely by chance; important in education because a single characteristic of a very large number of students, like their test scores or average grades or even height, approximates such a curve when graphed. Among other names for the curve are Gaussian curve, normal probability curve, normal frequency curve, normal curve, and, informally, bell-shaped curve. See grading on the curve.

normalize. In educational statistics, a technical term for adjusting a set of observational data such as test scores so that they more closely approximate a normal probability distribution. See normal distribution curve.

normal school. Obsolete term for an institution that provides pre-service teacher training.

norm-referenced test. Any standardized test provided with norms obtained in its standardization, so that scores on the test derive their meaning by reference to the norms; used to distinguish such tests from a criterion-referenced test, for which the scores derive their meaning instead by reference to specified criteria (or learning objectives) on which the test is based. See criterion-referenced test.

norms. With respect to standardized testing, extensive statistical findings that document how representative groups of students have actually performed on a standardized test; for adequate score interpretation, norms often need to be provided on bases that are nationwide, statewide, school-system-wide, and comparable to the students concerned in other essential respects such as socioeconomic status.

NSF. See National Science Foundation.

nuclear family. The basic conjugal family unit consisting of mother, father, and children, as distinct from the extended family. See extended family.

number facts. Facts concerning the numerals 0 through 9 or 10 when multiplied or added, or divided or subtracted, that are memorized in elementary school, such as $2 \times 1 = 2$, $2 \times 2 = 4$, $2 \times 3 = 6$, $2 \times 4 = 8$, and so on; frequently shown in tables, like the multiplication tables used in earlier decades. The four types of number facts learned are addition facts, subtraction facts, multiplication facts, and division facts.

numerical grading system. See grading system.

nursery school. A school for children of preschool ages, ranging from ages 2 or 3 through 4 or 5. See cooperative nursery school, day-care center, early childhood education, Montessori method.

nursing school. Informal term for a school providing education that prepares individuals for the nursing profession; a hospital nursing school is one attached to a hospital, as distinguished from a nursing school or program that is part of a college or university.

O

objectives approach. A viewpoint or method applied in a curriculum revision project in a school or school system; in it, detailed definitions are made of objectives such as the skills, abilities, knowledge, and attitudes to be developed in students, with the definitions often stated in the form of behavioral objectives. Materials and techniques for instruction and evaluation are then developed for realizing the objectives. See behavioral objectives.

objective test. 1. In psychological testing, any test for which the use of subjective judgment by test-scorers is virtually eliminated, so that qualified educators scoring the test independently would derive essentially the same scores. 2. Generally, any short-answer test scored with a key to the correct answers, and especially machine-scored standardized tests.

observational learning. Learning accomplished through watching an actual situation or a model performer.

observation of instruction. 1. The inspection of classroom teaching by a supervisor for such purposes as evaluation of teacher and pupil performance or diagnosis of instructional difficulties. 2. In professional teacher education, the witnessing of actual teaching situations in order to learn or evaluate techniques being demonstrated; also, a review of videotaped (or filmed) records of one's own teaching for purposes of learning and improvement.

occupational education. In some applications, refers to an emphasis on vocational skills and social accommodation in the teaching of mentally retarded students.

oceanography. The branch of the earth sciences concerned with the sea, including the marine aspects of geography, geology, physics, chemistry, biology (marine biology), and meteorology.

off-campus. Not on the campus of a college or school; can refer to almost any facility or activity, such as student housing, instructional sites, artistic performances, student employment, or student teaching experience (in teacher education).

old school tie. Figurative expression in the United States used to refer to alumni connections with a college or a preparatory school; derives from striped neckties bearing the individual school colors of the private secondary schools in Britain known as "public schools."

ombudsperson. A full-time officer at some secondary schools and other educational institutions who provides impartial services to review any grievances of students against the institution, and to present quasi-judicial recommendations for the just resolution of each grievance; senior teaching personnel frequently serve in such posts.

one-way observation facilities. Rooms having one or more walls outfitted with a device like a one-way vision mirror (which is seen as a mirror from inside the room but as a clear window from outside the room), so that class instruction or other activities can be studied without distraction of those being observed. Used especially in research concerning learning processes of young children.

on-the-job training. Training in the skills of a career or an occupation while the individual being trained is actually carrying out the work of an employed position.

ontogeny. A term in biology referring to the development or life cycle of the individual organism; often contrasted with phylogeny, the development of the type or species of organism.

ontology. An area of metaphysics concerned with the analysis or study of existence.

open admissions. A nonselective admissions process that makes higher education available to more students, usually by accepting applicants with any high-school diploma, or in some cases learning equivalent to the level of high-school graduation.

open book test. An examination in which students are permitted to use books or other reference materials while answering the examination questions.

open classroom. An innovative type of architectural design for classrooms of relatively wide interest in the 1960s; in it, instructional areas in an elementary school were not divided into walled classrooms of conventional size but were grouped in a large open space occupied by several classes each separated by bookshelves and other low partitions. Also called a classroom without walls. Differs from open education. See open education.

Open Corridor. The name of a widely influential program of open education conducted in a number of elementary schools in the New York City school system; it was introduced in the late 1960s under the leadership of Lillian Weber, an associate professor of elementary education at the City College of New York. See open education.

open education. A broad method of educating children that was widely adopted in elementary schools in the 1960s and 1970s; in an open education classroom, children learn at their own individual initiative in activity areas for such subjects as reading, writing, mathematics, science, nature, and art, with the teacher moving freely among them to guide their work and record their progress. The method was inspired largely by the approach used in the infant schools (for children aged 5–7) of Great Britain; it was at times referred to incorrectly by the term, open classroom (see open classroom).

open end formula. In public school finance, a policy of providing annual state aid to school districts under which aid is not limited to a ceiling amount but is furnished in whatever amount results from application of an authorized formula; appropriations by the legislature concerned are made not for a specified amount but for so much as will be needed to meet the formula requirements.

open enrollment. An unusual provision in the policy of a public school system in the United States under which children residing anywhere in the school district are permitted to attend one or more designated schools; contrasts with customary policy under which specific attendance zones are defined within the district for specific schools, and students attend only the school or schools serving their specific zones. See school attendance zone.

Open University. British university introduced in 1969 to serve the needs of adult learners with extensive coursework provided through TV, as well as by radio broadcasts and by correspondence study; most students are employed full-time, and meeting degree requirements involves little or no class attendance. See American Open University.

operational learning. The acquisition of skills and knowledge by practice or experience.

oral-aural. See audiolingual.

orals. 1. Informal term for any type of oral examinations. 2. Informal term for one of the few significant uses of oral examinations in education in the United States, when required for the Ph.D. (or another type of doctorate) at a number of universities: first, as "qualifying orals," and then as "defense of the thesis" orals given after the dissertation (thesis) is written.

orchestra. Group of student musicians playing orchestral instruments who constitute an official "school orchestra" or "college orchestra" representing the institution; such a student orchestra may be operated either as part of the music instructional program or an extracurricular activity.

organized play. Term used in schooling to distinguish between free play and either supervised play or play by the whole group in a game with rules.

orientation course. An introductory course designed to familiarize students with a particular subject area, and to help them plan for additional coursework in that area.

orientation program. An introductory program of talks and activities designed to help students become familiar with, and adjust to, a new educational setting such as a college or high school. Also called freshman orientation.

outcome. 1. A change resulting from learning that can be observed in the behavior of a student, as distinguished from an objective that is a sought-after result. 2. Loosely, the result of an educational program, the operation of a process, or a series of events.

outdoor education. An approach to education drawing substantially on interests arising in the environmental movement begun in the 1960s and heavily emphasizing field studies in the outdoors, ecological concerns, and natural resources.

out-of-state. At a state college or university, term used to refer to higher tuition fees or admissions standards applied to students whose legal residence is outside the state sponsoring the institution; also called nonresident.

outreach. Pertains to the provision of instruction, guidance, or other educational service in facilities outside the educational institution and in the community for easy access by persons needing the services.

Outward Bound. A program sponsored by an organization of that name providing young people with exploration and survival training in wilderness and outdoor settings, usually for several days at a time; was of relatively wide interest to adolescents in the 1960s and 1970s.

overachiever. A student whose academic performance is thought to exceed the evaluation and expectation of his or her potential.

overage in grade. An administrative term applied to a pupil who is notably older in age than most classmates who are in the same grade in school.

overhead projector. An audiovisual device especially popular in classroom teaching that projects images lettered or drawn on transparent sheets onto a screen or wall even in fully lighted rooms.

overlapping. Statistical term referring to the extent to which the distribution patterns of two sets of measurements, like test scores or course grades, overlap one another.

P

paired associate learning. Learning in which items are presented in pairs, and retention is then assessed by presenting one of the paired items and asking the student to respond with the other.

paradigm. 1. An ideal or near-ideal model or example. 2. In language study, an example showing conjugation of a word whereby the word undergoes changes in inflectional form to denote such elements as number, tense, person, and gender.

parallel-curriculum plan. A plan for elementary schooling used occasionally in the past, in which a school's pupils were divided into a slow group that finished the school's curriculum in eight years and a fast group that finished the curriculum in six years.

parallel play. Among preschool children, type of play engaged in by children too young for cooperative play; in parallel play, they use similar toys in much the same ways near each other but without interacting.

parameter. 1. In wide figurative use, a determining or limiting factor, as in a reference to the basic parameters of antiinflation policy. 2. In mathematics and statistics, a technical term for specific types of defining or determining factors.

paraprofessional. 1. In education, primarily a teacher aide; see teacher aide. 2. In the case of many professions, a person qualified by education and experience to work in an auxiliary or technical specialty related to the profession, in such capacities as a paralegal assistant in the law, physician's assistant in medicine, dental hygienist or dental assistant in dentistry, and engineering technician in engineering.

parental consent. In some cases a legal requirement for the protection of the school, representing written permission by the student's parent or guardian for the student to engage in a special activity, usually one falling outside regular school hours and taking place outside the school building.

parent association. An organization of the parents of the young people in a public school and in a public school system, to which teachers do not also belong as in a PTA; parent associations have developed in some school systems after teachers have withdrawn from PTAs as a result of labor-management disputes between the teachers and the school system administration.

parent conference. Informal term for a meeting by a teacher or other school officer with the parent of a student in order to discuss the student, either for a regular informational session or a special problem. Also called teacher-parent conference or parent-teacher conference.

Parent's Confidential Statement (PCS). Blank form employed by the College Scholarship Service of The College Board from the 1950s through the 1970s for collecting family financial information used in estimating the financial need of applicants for financial aid; succeeded by the Financial Aid Form (FAF). See Financial Aid Form.

parents' night. In elementary and secondary schooling, an annual occasion at which a school invites parents to visit the school, meet with teachers, and view displays exhibited by students.

Parent-Teacher Association (PTA). Joint organization of parents and teachers for each public school and community that is also linked to state and national levels of the National Congress of Parents and Teachers, with central offices in Chicago, Illinois.

parent-teacher association. An association of parents and teachers for a school or community that is not affiliated with the National Congress of Parents and Teachers.

parochial school. 1. Broadly, a private elementary or secondary school operated by a religious organization, such as a parish of a religious faith. **2.** As widely understood, an elementary or secondary school sponsored by the Roman Catholic church.

part-time. As applying to a student, enrollment in studies on less than a full-time basis; as applying to a teacher, employed for teaching on less than a full-time basis. See full-time.

pass. 1. To obtain credit or other recognition as a student for meeting at least minimum requirements by performing in a test, an assignment, or other studies above the level of a failing grade or mark. See grading system. **2.** In elementary school especially, a written authorization for the pupil to leave his or her assigned classroom on an errand.

pass-fail grading system. See grading system.

passing grade, passing mark. A grade or mark for performance as a student in a course, test, or assignment above failing or failure. See grading system.

passive-aggressive child. In child psychology, a type of personality in which normal feelings of anger and hostility are repressed but which find expression in school in hidden, disruptive ways.

P.A. system. See public-address system.

patrol, safety patrol. A group of older students in a school appointed to promote compliance with safety regulations on school buses and at crosswalks and intersections.

patterned responses. Desired responses elicited by the use of different patterns and forms of stimuli; used especially in behavior modification. See also conditioned reflex.

Pavlov, Ivan Petrovich (1849–1936). Russian physiologist and experimental psychologist, best known for his discovery of the conditioned reflex in his work with dogs; prepared the way for behaviorism and modern learning theory. See also conditioning.

P.E. Informal, widely used abbreviation for physical education; see physical education.

Peace Corps. A federal program established in 1961 under President John F. Kennedy that trained and sent volunteers for tours of duty abroad to work with communities in developing countries on agricultural, technological, and educational programs.

pedagogy. Older term for the practice or profession of teaching, now somewhat pedantic.

pedantic. Person or manner characterized by an unnecessary and exaggerated display of learning, or by minute and meaningless academic formalism.

pediatrics. The science concerned with the medical care and diseases of children.

peer group. See peer influence.

peer influence. The effect on a child's thinking and behavior of other children about the same age or developmental level with whom the child associates; those associates are also called the child's peer group.

Pell Grant. See Basic Educational Opportunity Grant Program.

PEP. See American College Testing Program.

pep rally. An enthused student meeting led by coaches and cheerleaders and held before a sports competition to stir school spirit and boost the morale of the team.

percentage grading system. See grading system.

percentile. A type of scale widely used to compare relative standings between students, particularly with respect to test scores. A percentile standing is reported as an ordinal number from 1st through 99th, and is read as follows: a standing at the 87th percentile means standing ahead of 87% of the persons in a specific reference group (one that is always identified with the reporting of percentiles); a standing at the 72nd percentile means standing or rank ahead of 72% of those in the reference group. Percentile results for a person or group are also called percentile ranks or percentile scores.

perception. **1.** The faculty of an individual resulting in accurate detection of significant or desired aspects of external reality through the senses. **2.** A mental image or observation of external reality detected through the senses. **3.** An insight or intuition.

perceptual discrimination. **1.** The act of identifying and differentiating between things perceived. **2.** In reading, the ability to perceive distinguishing features of symbols.

perennialism. A twentieth-century educational philosophy of which Robert M. Hutchins was a leading exponent; in it, truth and knowledge as represented in traditional liberal arts and sciences learning are held to be permanent and universal, and hence fundamental in education.

performance. The carrying out of work by a student in an actual assignment, test, or course.

performance-based education. See competency-based education.

performance-based teacher education. An emphasis in professional teacher education on actual demonstration of teaching practices to provide evidence of what the individual teacher knows and can accomplish.

performance contract. See contract learning.

performance test. **1.** Used at times to refer to a test consisting mainly of nonverbal test questions; see nonverbal test questions. **2.** Loosely applied to an examination consisting of tasks to be performed manually (rather than of questions to be answered) or of some genuine functional tasks, as with a road test for the driver's license.

Peripatetic School. **1.** The name given to the school in ancient Athens where Aristotle taught while pacing up and down the covered walks of the Lyceum, followed by his pupils. **2.** Teaching or performing that is done while walking back and forth.

permanent certificate, permanent license. See certification.

permanent record. For a student, extensive records of grades received, test results, health records, counseling and disciplinary sessions, home and personal life, and any other relevant matters that are kept on a long-term basis by the school; access to information in such records is controlled by the student and his or her family. See Family Educational Rights and Privacy Act.

permanent substitute. A teacher hired on a permanent full-time basis as a substitute.

permissive. Tending to let one or more children behave with a considerable amount of freedom that others responsible for children might not allow, as with a permissive grandfather.

per-pupil cost. For a public school district, an accounting statistic usually calculated by dividing the annual current expenditures by the number of pupils in average daily attendance; the figure is widely viewed as an approximate index of the comparative quality of education provided by school districts.

personal days. For public school teachers, days on which a teacher may legitimately be absent from regular duties in order to attend to personal business. See professional days.

personal guidance. See guidance.

personality. The total, integrated pattern of mental, emotional, and social qualities of an individual.

personnel director. In a public school system, an administrative officer responsible for hiring school personnel, keeping personnel records,

dismissal, changes or transfers, and all procedures pertinent to employment. Responsible usually to the superintendent of schools. The
position title is also termed director of personnel.

Pestalozzi, Johann Heinrich (1746-1827). Swiss educator and re-
former whose theories are widely considered fundamental to elementary education as practiced today.

Ph.D. See Doctor of Philosophy.

phenomenology. 1. The analysis of phenomena in philosophy. **2.** A
school of philosophic thought founded by Edmund Husserl (1859–
1938) and concerned with consciousness and the experiencing of
phenomena.

Phi Beta Kappa. The major honorary society for college students who
attain very high academic averages after at least three years of full-
time bachelor's-degree study; name also applied to an individual member of the society, which was founded in 1776 and began the tradition
of collegiate fraternities in American colleges.

philosophy. 1. The academic discipline broadly consisting of rational
analysis of all aspects of reality and existence, and viewed by scholars
today as having among its major branches the fields of logic, epistemology, ethics, aesthetics, and metaphysics. **2.** The underlying theory
or basis in philosophic thought of any area or discipline, such as the
philosophy of education. **3.** As informally applied to individuals,
the person's fundamental beliefs about existence and conduct.

philosophy of education. See philosophy.

phonetics. The science or study of the sounds in human speech, or
any broad application or branch of the field. See also phonics method.

phonics method. The broad method for the teaching of reading that
is based on learning how to sound out letters and letter-patterns in
words. Also referred to as phonetic or phonetics method, or ABC
method or alphabet method.

phylogeny. A term in biology referring to the evolutionary development of a type of organism, such as a species or genus; often contrasted with ontogeny, the development of the individual organism.

physical education. Instruction designed to foster body development, motor skills, abilities in athletics, and good health through physical fitness. In elementary grades, emphasis in the subject is usually on muscle tone, body movement, and fitness. In secondary school, students may frequently engage in sports such as soccer, basketball, or swimming.

physical sciences. Any of the sciences such as chemistry, physics, or geology dealing with the nature, physical composition, and structure of nonliving matter.

physics. A branch of physical science that deals with the scientific study of the nature, properties, and interaction of energy and matter.

Piaget, Jean (1896–1981). Swiss psychologist, best known for his work with children and their cognitive development; in his theories, such development is determined genetically and proceeds in stages that always follow the same sequential order. Among his writings are *Structuralism* (1971), *The Mechanisms of Perception* (1969), and *The Growth of Logical Thinking* (1958).

pidgin. A form of spoken language comprising two or more regular languages, as with pidgin English developed in parts of Asia and Africa; used in communication between groups who speak different languages.

pilot program. A new endeavor or project being tried out in an early operational form.

placement. 1. The assignment of a student to an appropriate level and type of instruction, as in the placement of a transfer pupil in grade 3 or of an entering college student in third-year French. See also advanced placement. **2.** Services provided by institutions of higher education and postsecondary education to assist students in finding employment; student placement services or offices seek to help students find temporary positions while continuing their studies, and career placement services help graduating students or graduates find permanent career positions. Also called college placement services, offices, or bureaus.

plagiarize. The act of stealing ideas or writings from another and representing them as one's own. In education, students who plagiarize in compositions are usually given failing marks and otherwise punished.

plan book. A notebook used by the teacher for recording teaching activities projected for such specified times as the day, the week, and the month. See also lesson plan.

plateau. See learning plateau.

Plato. 1. Greek philosopher, died 347 B.C. (birth year uncertain, but around 430 B.C.); founded a school, the "Academy," in Athens, and taught mathematics and philosophy there. A disciple of Socrates and author of works in the form of Socratic dialogues that have exerted great influence in philosophic and religious thought. **2.** A major system of computer-assisted instruction developed by the Control Data Corporation; commercially available to schools and companies with a wide variety of courses for education and training.

play. See free play, organized play, parallel play, play hooky, play school, play therapy.

play hooky. Colloquial term for being truant (absent from school without parental consent); also given as hookey.

play school. A nursery school for children of preschool age emphasizing play activities for the children rather than educational activities.

play therapy. The use of toys, games, and materials specifically designed for diagnosis and treatment of mentally or emotionally disturbed children usually between the ages of 3–10.

pledge. 1. A student accepted as a candidate for membership in a college fraternity or sorority, but not yet initiated as a member.

2. On the part of a college student, to accept an offer by a fraternity or sorority to become a candidate for membership.

pocket calculator. A small electronic or mechanical device with a keyboard on which to perform arithmetic and mathematical operations; used widely in mathematics, science, and business classes.

point-credit value. Value of degree credits assigned to a course or courses; such credits are sometimes called points, point-credits, or credit-points at colleges and universities. See credits.

police science. See law enforcement.

political science. A field of the social sciences that deals with government; synonymous with government as the name of an academic discipline.

polytechnic. Refers to a school that specializes in technology and applied science, especially engineering.

population education. Teaching and learning concerned with the processes and characteristics of population, especially in connection with the current rapid increase in world population called the population explosion.

positive reinforcement. See programmed instruction.

positive transfer. See transfer of learning.

postdoctoral learning. Research and study beyond the doctoral degree, generally on specific projects.

postgraduate. In British university systems, study on a level past the bachelor's degree, which is termed the "graduate" level of study in the United States.

postsecondary education. Education beyond secondary school graduation, including higher education in colleges and universities and diverse forms of occupational or vocational education, career education, technical education, continuing education, adult education, and lifelong learning.

posttest. See pretest.

practical. In connection with knowledge, useful or applied, as differentiated from theoretical and disinterested.

practice. 1. Repeated exercise of specific learnings or skills in order to improve retention and proficiency. 2. Application of knowledge in a functional situation; to put knowledge into practice. 3. A customary manner of carrying out some process or operation, as in a teaching practice.

practicum. 1. A course or student exercise involving practical experience as well as theoretical study. 2. Supervised experience in counseling as part of professional preservice education of counselors.

pragmatism. An American school of thought in philosophy emphasizing the importance of validating conceptions and truth in action or by their practical consequences.

preadolescence. The period of a few years in life just before puberty, around the ages of 11 to 13.

preceptor, preceptress. A generally archaic term for a tutor, instructor, or teacher.

précis. A concise summary or digest of a longer written work.

precocious child. A child who is impressively advanced for his or her age in at least some types of accomplishment. Sometimes also called a gifted child, or superior child.

prefect. The title of various kinds of administrative officers at some schools and colleges of the Roman Catholic church, as with a prefect of studies responsible for curricular supervision at a parochial secondary school.

prelaw. A four-year bachelor's-degree program in higher education that prepares students for law school; emphasis is on history, government, and philosophy, often, though, preparatory subject requirements for law school allow wide flexibility.

Preliminary Scholastic Aptitude Test-National Merit Scholarship Qualifying Test (PSAT-NMSQT). A two-hour version of the Scholastic Aptitude Test (SAT) of The College Board that is also provided by the Board and is given by secondary schools on one Saturday every October for interested students in grade 11; offered to furnish relatively inexpensive early versions of likely SAT scores and practice for the SAT, it is also required as the initial qualifying test in the National Merit Scholarship Program. See The College Board, National Merit Scholarship Program, Scholastic Aptitude Test.

premed. Pertaining to a four-year bachelor's degree program in college that prepares students for medical school; in it, emphasis is on the natural sciences and broad liberal arts.

preparatory school. A private secondary school preparing students for college.

Prep for Prep. A program sponsored by a nonprofit organization named Broad Jump that offers enrichment in secondary schooling to minority-group children who are gifted and highly motivated; approximately twenty private schools have participated in the program by each reserving places for from one to five program students a year. Participating schools in the New York City area have included Dalton, Brearley, Trinity, and Fieldston.

preppy. 1. Colloquial term for a student at a preparatory school, derived from the term prep school; see preparatory school. **2.** Characteristic of prep school students and of their families, in whimsical, colloquial references.

preprimer. A reading textbook designed for use by beginning readers and limited to a vocabulary of very few words given in very short sentences.

prep school. Colloquial term for a private preparatory school; see preparatory school.

prerequisite. A requirement that must be met prior to acceptance of a student into some activity; most often, consists of a stipulated course that must be completed before one may enroll in a succeeding course.

preschool education. Education for children from the ages of about 2 through 4 or 5, before entering kindergarten or grade 1 in elementary school.

prescriptive teaching. See diagnostic-prescriptive teaching.

press. See university press.

pretest. 1. In an educational experiment, the administration of standardized or other tests at the start of the experiment in order to obtain evaluations with which results of a similar "posttest" at the end of the experiment may be compared. **2.** In standardized test development, early administration of a test form or test items in order to ascertain by statistical findings how the form or items function.

primary grade. Generally, a grade from kindergarten through grade 3 inclusively in elementary school.

primary school. Informal term for an elementary school. See elementary school.

primary source. See secondary source.

primer. A reading textbook normally intended for pupils early in grade 1; may be preceded in a basic reading series by a preprimer.

principal. The chief administrator of a public school; originally derived from the term, principal teacher. In some cases, also used as a title for high-ranking administrative officers of school systems.

privacy of student records. See Family Educational Rights and Privacy Act.

private. When referring to an educational institution, as in "private school" or "private college," an institution sponsored and financed under private auspices rather than by a governmental body.

probation. 1. In a school or college, student status in which the student continues studies on a trial basis; probation is usually disciplinary, for reasons of either poor academic performance or disruptive conduct, with the student allowed to go off probation upon meeting specified conditions. **2.** In juvenile court, a state of suspended sentence in which a delinquent is allowed to go on parole.

problem child. A child who has emotional difficulties, reflected in seriously disruptive behavior in school that compromises learning, achievement, and social adjustment.

process-centered education. An educational system that emphasizes the process of individual learning and development of cognitive skills regardless of subject matter taught including such skills as analysis, inference, classification, and measurement.

proctor. A person who supervises or helps supervise the giving of an examination.

professional accreditation. See accreditation.

professional days. For public school teachers, days on which a teacher may legitimately be absent from regular duties for purposes of professional enrichment, as when attending in-service training programs or professional meetings. See personal days.

professional fraternity. A society open to men and women whose members are in a specific professional area such as education, and whose purpose is to promote the further development and improvement of the profession.

professional school. In higher education, a school providing education that qualifies students for a profession.

professional teacher education. See teacher education.

professor. Title given to the higher-ranking scholars in full-time positions of teaching or research at an institution of higher education. "Professor" is normally the title of the highest rank of such faculty members. Other ranks in descending order are denoted by the titles of "associate professor," "assistant professor," and "instructor." Tenure accompanies the higher ranks from the level of assistant or associate professor up at a number of institutions. See also adjunct professor, distinguished professor, lecturer, visiting professor.

proficiency. Accomplishment or expertness in a subject, body of skills, or other area.

Proficiency Examination Program (PEP). See American College Testing Program.

profile. Term used to refer to a graph of a set of characteristics, such as a student's results on a battery of achievement tests in numerous subjects, or the average grades of all the students in a class.

prognostic test. A test seeking to measure characteristics that attempt to predict successful outcomes of educational programs.

program. 1. An organized body of educational offerings, like the courses in a school of business that represent its accounting program, or the numerous degree sequences and many courses at a university constituting its program or programs in the arts; all the educational offerings of an institution, representing its program of studies. 2. The set of courses in which a student registers for a term or year. 3. Curricula or sets of courses to be taken by a student that lead to differing types of concentrations, diplomas, degrees, or degree majors, such as the college-preparatory diploma program, the general diploma program, the program leading to the bachelor's degree in mechanical engineering, or the program for a bachelor's degree with a major in sociology. 4. A plan for carrying on certain activities or attaining certain goals or objectives. 5. The events planned for a performance or public gathering, or a printed statement of such events and accompanying notes. 6. A unit of programmed instruction. 7. A set of instructions to control the operations of a computer system.

programmed instruction. 1. Originally, instruction by "teaching machines" of the type widely popularized by behavioral psychologists in the 1950s, notably B. F. Skinner. **2.** Instructional material written in the step-by-step form that is based on the learning theories which also underlie teaching machines; such material typically includes in each step a comprehensible, new item of knowledge to be learned, a question about it that is easy to answer correctly, and prompt confirmation of the answer's correctness to give "positive reinforcement" to consolidate learning. **3.** An educational technique using such instructional material.

programming. 1. Preparing sets of coded instructions to control the operations of a computer system. **2.** Planning any other type of program.

progressive education. A widely influential movement in American education that gathered momentum with formation of the Progressive Education Association in 1919; among basic elements of its approach were accommodation of schooling to individual differences between children, belief that children learn best when pursuing their individual interests and by actual performance or action, and provision for flexibility and initiative in learning on the part of the child. John Dewey was a leader of the movement in theory and practice. With many of its reforms established in a number of schools, it essentially ended as a distinct movement in the 1950s but its influence continued in later movements and developments.

progressive school. In former decades, term for a school that used an approach like that of the progressive education movement in its teaching.

project. For students, an assignment or task of some special kind that may be intended either for a group of pupils or the individual student.

projective test. A personality assessment device in psychological testing for which the professional test-giver asks the individual test-taker to interpret a picture or other stimulus that has no obvious meaning, as with the Rorschach ink blots.

prom. In secondary and higher education, a formal dance held at the end of the junior year (junior prom), and at the end of the senior year (senior prom),usually in a commercial establishment such as a restaurant or night club.

promotion. 1. For a pupil, the action by the school of being advanced at the end of a school year to the next higher grade level; sometimes termed academic promotion when done in the normal circumstances of satisfactory or better scholastic performance by the student in the current grade level. See also automatic promotion, grade level, grade retention, grade skipping, nongraded class, passing. 2. Advancement in position on the part of a person in employment.

proof. 1. In logic, demonstration by established principles that a conclusion follows inescapably from given premises. 2. Similar demonstration of the validity of a conclusion in another field, such as mathematics, one of the sciences, or law.

proposition. 1. In mathematics, a theorem to be demonstrated or problem to be performed. 2. In logic, an assertion that may be analyzed as either true or false.

proprietary school. A private school chartered as a profit-making organization; postsecondary institutions providing noncollegiate instruction in occupational or technical fields are frequently proprietary.

proseminar. In higher education, a course operated with much tutorial study as in a graduate seminar but open to junior-year or senior-year undergraduates of high academic ability.

provisional certificate, provisional license. See certification.

provost. Title sometimes used for a high-ranking administrative officer at a university.

PSAT. See Preliminary Scholastic Aptitude Test.

psycholinguistics. The psychology of language; study of the psychological processes involved in language and communication as they relate to other activities.

psychological services. Term sometimes used for the counseling, testing, and diagnostic services offered by a high school or college as part of its student-personnel services.

psychological test. Broad term referring to any type of standardized test, interest inventory, personality evaluative instrument, or other device developed with the techniques of the specialty of tests and measurements in psychology.

psychology. 1. The academic discipline constituting the science of the mind and of mental activity or of patterns of behavior; classified with the natural sciences or social sciences. **2.** The study of this science in connection with a field or group, as with educational psychology, child psychology, or adolescent psychology. See also educational psychology.

psychometrics. The specialty of tests and measurements in psychology; psychological testing.

psychomotor. Refers to the conscious control of muscular movement, as in the psychomotor development of infants.

psychotherapy. Professional treatment to improve mental health or social adjustment; also often called simply therapy.

PTA. See Parent-Teacher Association.

puberty. The transitional time in the life cycle marked by the maturity of the reproductive organs and the emergence of secondary sexual characteristics at the start of adolescence around the age of 12 or 13.

public. When referring to an educational institution, as in "public school" or "public college," an institution sponsored and financed by a state, county, or other governmental unit rather than under private auspices.

public-address system (P.A. system). Equipment including one or more loudspeakers and microphones enabling a speaker to address a large group; may be installed in a school building so that a speaker in the principal's office may address groups in all classrooms at once, or may be used in an auditorium or at an outdoor gathering.

public education. 1. The extensive system of government-sponsored elementary and secondary schools attended without charge in the United States. **2.** Any program or institution of education provided by a government body.

public school. 1. In the United States, an elementary or secondary school operated as part of a public school system or district and supported by taxes to provide education to any child of eligible age and residence without charge. **2.** In Great Britain, one of a number of privately endowed boarding and day schools providing secondary education in university-preparatory studies.

pupil. A younger child attending school, usually elementary school; also, a synonym for student, or an older term for a person of any age being taught in individual private lessons as with singing or instrumental performance in music.

pupil-personnel services. See student-personel services.

pupil-teacher ratio. See student-teacher ratio.

pure research. See basic research.

PUSH-EXCEL Program. A program for minority-group students founded by Reverend Jesse L. Jackson in 1976 to stimulate motivation in the students; operates demonstration centers in major cities where program representatives work with students to instill self-confidence, self-discipline, good work habits, and determination to avoid taking drugs. Also known as Push for Excellence, the program has been aided by federal funds.

Push for Excellence. See PUSH-EXCEL Program.

Pygmalion phenomenon. Informal term referring to an apparent effect of expectancy on the part of the teacher on pupil development; those pupils for whom the teacher has higher expectations seem actually to attain higher development even when the pupils do not differ in initial ability from their classmates. Term stems from its introduction in the 1968 book, *Pygmalion in the Classroom*, by Robert Rosenthal and Lenore Jacobson.

Q

qualifying examination. 1. An examination through which the student is required to qualify for going on to some segment of further studies, as in a professional study program. 2. See orals.

quality-point values. A special set of values assigned to its courses usually by a college in addition to (and similar in purpose to) the point-credit values assigned courses for use in defining academic degree requirements. See credits.

quantitative mental ability. General ability or aptitude at working with numerical concepts or mathematics, in the terminology used for some psychological tests.

quarter. In the academic-year schedule of institutions of higher education operating on a quarter-system calendar, a term some three months long with three quarters making up the normal academic year of formal instruction running approximately from September to June; a summer quarter for additional course offerings may feature special terms of shorter length.

quarter-hour credits. Units of degree credits assigned to courses at colleges and universities operating on quarter-system calendars; generally, 1.5 quarter-hour credits are equivalent to 1 semester-hour credit. See credits, quarter, semester-hour credits.

quartile. A unit in a four-unit scale, on which rank-order standings of students according to indices such as grades or test scores may be given as standings by quartile or fourths; for instance, a student in the top 25% in some respect like class rank stands in the top quartile.

question banks. Collections of questions for use in psychological tests; see item bank.

quiz. 1. Informal term for a test, especially a short, minor one. 2. To question one or more persons briefly on some topic.

quota. An allocated portion or share; in education, such an allocation set in advance in such connections as the enrollment limit for a certain course or program, or the acceptances of applicants having various kinds of backgrounds in selective admissions.

quotient score. A type of test score like the obsolescent ratio intelligence quotient score, relating the individual's performance level to the typical or average performance level for comparable individuals of various ages; to derive such a score, the person's test results are converted to a score expressed as an age in years and months, and this score is divided by the individual's chronological age in years and months as a step toward obtaining the eventual quotient score. See Intelligence Quotient (IQ).

R

racial balance. See integration.

racial integration. See integration.

R and D. See research and development.

random error. 1. In the teaching of reading, one of varying mistakes made by a pupil in reading aloud that occurs without pattern, as distinguished from systematic errors. 2. In a process of statistical evaluation like testing, an error due solely to chance that does not substantially change the general import of a large number of obtained scores or other values.

range. The span on a scale across which some set of values is distributed, as with the ages of pupils in a class, course grades, or test scores; in statistics, consists of the difference between the smallest and largest values or of that difference plus one.

rank. The relative standing of an individual with respect to some index of performance or characteristic in an identified group of comparable individuals, such as rank in class (numerical standing among classmates on the basis of grade-point average) or the individual's national percentile rank on a specific test score. See class rank, grade-point average, percentile.

rating. 1. A judgmental appraisal of given characteristics made in a systematic way, as in ratings of personal qualities of college admissions applicants made by guidance counselors or ratings of teacher performance made by supervisors. **2.** A military specialty of persons in the U.S. Armed Forces, entered by enlisted personnel in the Navy and Marine Corps, or secured by Air Force personnel in such areas as bombardment, navigation, and radar.

rating scale. A form with directions or similar device to provide a systematic approach in the making of ratings; as an example, a scale for rating a teacher may provide means for comparing the observed performance of one teacher with the performance of other teachers or with defined standards.

ratiocination. Reasoning, especially with the use of logic; see reasoning.

rationale. **1.** An explanation of underlying principles of a belief, action, project, or inquiry. **2.** A justification for some practice or course of action.

rationalism. **1.** A philosophical viewpoint holding that reason can serve as a source of knowledge without reliance on experience; a related view that reason and experience provide better means than irrational methods for validating knowledge and guiding conduct. **2.** In religion, a conviction that religious beliefs should be consistent with reason.

raw score. In standardized testing, the actual count of questions answered correctly by an examinee out of the total questions on the test; derived for conversion of the raw score to a type of score used in reporting the test results, such as a scaled score or national percentile score.

readability formula. One of a number of systematized methods for calculating an index of readability for a given body of reading material in prose, and for using the index to estimate for which grade level or age level of typical readers that material would be most appropriate; among widely used formulae are ones known as Washburne-Vogel, Lorge, Yoakam, Flesch, and Dale-Chall. Formulae take into account such factors as average number of syllables per word and average number of words per sentence and are based on extensive research.

readability index. See readability formula.

readiness. 1. In learning generally, the stage of individual development at which abilities, skills, and interests have matured sufficiently to enable the individual to successfully acquire certain new skills and knowledge; especially significant varieties of readiness in education are reading readiness and writing readiness on the part of young children. **2.** A similar state or stage of receptivity of an individual with respect to any endeavor or experience, such as career selection.

reading comprehension. The extent to which an individual understands material that has been read and is able to recall both such meaning and factual details of the reading; such capabilities are evaluated on a reading comprehension test.

reading consultant. A teaching specialist in a school system or school who is primarily responsible for helping to improve classroom instruction in reading.

reading difficulty. 1. For a particular reading selection or passage, the quality of proving hard or laborious for certain students to read. See readability formula. **2.** A deficiency in a student who finds reading abnormally laborious and unpleasant. **3.** See also reading power.

reading disability. See dyslexia.

reading laboratory. A classroom, library room, or other facility at a school or college with special equipment and instruction to help students improve their reading skills and reading speed and comprehension, and to provide help in both remedial and developmental instruction; also, a series of boxed sets of multilevel materials serving as the reading textbook for the class in each successive grade.

reading level. 1. For a student, the level of reading capability developed to the present by the student; assessed either by the grade level of reading textbooks in which the student is currently succeeding, or by standardized tests; on tests, commonly expressed as reading above or below the average level for the student's grade on national norms. See grade-equivalent score. 2. For a written passage or work, the typical school grades or age-span of readers for whom the material is best suited.

reading power. The ability of a student to comprehend text of a given level of readability or difficulty, as assessed on a type of test named Degrees of Reading Power (DRP) that was developed in the late 1970s by the New York State Education Department and is published by The College Board; scores are reported on a special scale of 0 to 100 DRP Units, and commonly encountered prose passages range in readability from a low of about 25 DRP Units to a high of about 85 DRP Units.

reading rate. An individual's speed in reading with adequate comprehension, normally expressed in number of words per minute.

reading readiness. See readiness.

reason. 1. The power of understanding, deducing, and thinking, particularly in a rational, systematic manner; intellectual faculty through which knowledge is acquired. 2. An explanation, justification, or cause.

reasoning. 1. The act of applying reason or the reasoning powers to make inferences and derive conclusions. 2. An example of thus applying reason such as the reasoning presented to a court by a defense attorney.

recess. In elementary schooling, a short period of about a quarter-hour provided in both morning and afternoon schedules during which the pupils are released from class and usually engage in free play in the schoolyard or school gym and discharge physical energy.

recitation. Traditional term for a sustained, spoken response by the student in class after the teacher has asked the student to report on the day's assignment or present some information or explanation concerning a matter under study before the class.

recognition day. A ceremony held by some schools on a day near the end of the school year in which promotions of pupils to their next grade levels are announced, and selected pupils who have made special accomplishments receive recognition in the form of certificates and prizes.

recreation. In higher education, a field of study in physical education that prepares students for directing organized leisure-time programs; courses in the field cover such topics as community finances, facilities, and helping to develop recreational skills in the community.

reentry student. A student in secondary or higher education who returns to formal schooling to complete requirements for a diploma or degree, after having dropped out for a length of time.

reference book. Book containing specialized information that is designed to be consulted at random rather than read from start to finish. Among many types of reference books important in education are dictionaries, encyclopedias, atlases, almanacs, and directories.

reformatory. See reform school.

reform school. A penal institution for juvenile delinquents and first offenders where they receive training and rehabilitative services; also called a reformatory. See also correctional education.

refresher course. 1. A type of course designed especially to renew the knowledge of persons having prior familiarity with the subject. 2. Any course taken by a person for the purpose of renewing prior knowledge of the subject.

regent. 1. At some state universities or state systems of higher education, the title used for a member of the controlling board. 2. In New York State, the title used for a member of the unique state governmental board empowered to control public and private higher education in the state as well as all public and private schools in the state and other cultural institutions such as libraries and museums; the official name of this body is The Regents of the University of the State of New York.

Regents Examination. One of the large body of examinations offered for use by secondary schools throughout New York State by the Regents of the University of the State of New York through the State Education Department; each Regents examination covers the work of a course of subject in secondary school. Regents examinations are required for an optional graduation credential, the Regents high school diploma; introduced in 1864, the examinations were important especially in past eras for helping assure sound minimum standards in high-school instruction throughout the state.

regional accreditation. See accreditation.

register. Most notably in education, the act of enrolling in a school or college, or in one or more courses.

Registered Nurse (RN). A person who graduates from one of the following postsecondary programs and passes state RN examinations: an associate's-degree program normally completed in two years of full-time study; a diploma program widely conducted by hospital schools of nursing (generally takes three years' study); or a bachelor's-degree program in nursing offered by many four-year colleges.

registrar. The officer at an institution of higher education responsible for the keeping of all student records.

registration. The process provided for enrolling; see register.

released time. See religious instruction.

reliability. 1. The degree to which a psychological test can be depended on to produce consistent results in repeated uses; results on tests with relatively low reliability can vary widely just by chance. Expressed statistically by a reliability coefficient. 2. In general, trustworthiness.

reliability coefficient. See reliability.

religious instruction. Instruction of students in their religious faith, generally on a weekly basis, in a church or synagogue; students are excused from school attendance on what is sometimes called "released time" in instances when religious instruction is required during school hours.

remedial. Pertains to special instruction for some pupils that is designed to overcome any relatively minor learning deficiencies or difficulties, as, for example, in remedial reading, rather than to offset any severe disabilities or handicaps in general ability.

remedial reading. Pertains to the teaching of reading to pupils whose reading ability is generally below average, by means of identifying their difficulties and attempting to correct them. Most schools have special remedial reading classes, sections, and/or teachers.

repeater. Term referring to a pupil who failed in a previous term and is repeating a grade or a course.

report card. The time-honored type of form recording the student's subject grades, absences, and tardiness, and behavior ratings at the end of each marking period, that the young person brings home and often has signed by parents.

representative stage. In the artistic development of a child, the period in which he or she tries to draw things as they appear realistically, occurring after about age 5 or 6.

research. A process of systematic inquiry, investigation, and analysis of data in order to increase knowledge, test hypotheses, and arrive at conclusions.

research and development. Term used mainly in industry denoting the use of basic and applied research in order to develop new products and processes; referred to as "R and D."

research assistant. See assistant.

research paper. Most often, a composition that the student is expected to base very extensively on library research, and that accordingly includes numerous citations and footnotes with a bibliography.

Reserve Officers' Training Corps (ROTC). An organization of the United States Department of Defense having units at each of several hundred private and public colleges and universities: students accepted for the units receive financial aid and military training in addition to continuing in regular full-time studies, and normally qualify for reserve officer commissions on graduation; units are attached either to the Army (Army ROTC), the Air Force (AFROTC), or the Navy (NROTC).

residence requirements. Requirements set by a college or university of the least time a student must be enrolled in order to receive a degree from the institution, usually one or two academic years. Has no connection with the state resident requirements of state universities concerning lower tuition fees and preferential admissions consideration. See nonresident.

resident assistant. See resident counselor.

resident counselor. An upperclassman or graduate student living in a dormitory at a college or university and responsible for advising and guiding especially younger students in the dormitory; the counselor or advisor is usually compensated by receiving room and board free or at reduced rates.

residential school. See boarding school.

resource person. 1. An individual with special knowledge or background related to a topic under study by a class and whom the teacher asks to give a talk on that topic to the class or otherwise assist the class. **2.** A consultant with a special background who is assisting at a professional workshop.

resource units. A pool of teaching materials, methods, procedures, and information on different topics that are available to teachers in planning and developing courses.

résumé. A written summary of one's biographical, educational, and career qualifications, presented to a prospective employer. Also called curriculum vitae.

Rhodes Scholarship. A two-year scholarship named for Cecil Rhodes, nineteenth-century explorer in South Africa, and awarded by the Rhodes Trust, an educational foundation, for postgraduate studies at Oxford University to students from Great Britain, the U.S., and occasionally West Germany. More than 60 scholarships are awarded annually.

retarded child. A slow-learning child whose mental abilities and emotional development are extremely low as characterized by slow maturation, deficient intellectual functioning, inadequate social adjustment, and generally backward behavior. Special education or special schooling is generally required for such a child. See mentally retarded.

RN. See Registered Nurse.

retention. 1. Broadly, remembering or memorizing. 2. Rather rarely, used to refer to the practice of not promoting a student to the next higher grade at the end of a school year; see promotion.

retest. A repeated administration of an examination, either with an alternative and essentially equivalent form of the original test or with the same form and all other testing conditions remaining the same.

revenue sharing. A means of federal tax support in which a portion of federal tax revenues is provided to state and local governments for locally operated public-service programs including ones in education.

reverse discrimination. See Bakke decision.

review. 1. The process of refreshing one's knowledge of material already learned, often as preparation for a test. 2. An appraisal of a book, play, film, dance or musical performance, or art exhibition that is normally written for publication rather than student practice.

rhetoric. 1. Classic term for the art of speaking and writing well. 2. Overelaborate or insincere speech or writing.

right to privacy. See Family Educational Rights and Privacy Act.

Ritalin. One of the more widely used stimulant drugs given to hyperkinetic children that has the paradoxical effect of somewhat quieting their behavior and making it easier for them to learn; among other such drugs are dexedrine and methylphenidate. See hyperkinetic child.

role model. An individual whose role another chooses to emulate. Teachers may occasionally recognize role models among students.

role-playing. 1. In instruction, a technique in which pupils spontaneously enact assigned roles in a given historical, literary, or contemporary situation in order to understand that situation more thoroughly. 2. In counseling, a technique in which persons being counseled act out situations like those in real life in order to develop insights and express emotions.

roll. The attendance list for a class, course, or institution identifying the individuals who are officially registered. See call the roll.

rolling admission. A procedure followed by some colleges and universities whereby they evaluate an applicant's credentials when received, make a decision, and notify the applicant immediately rather than waiting until a fixed date in early spring to notify all applicants at the same time. See candidates' reply date agreement.

Romance Languages. Languages that are derived from Latin such as French, Spanish, Italian, Portuguese, and Rumanian.

roommate. A person with whom one shares a dormitory room or other living quarters.

root. In the study of English, that portion of a word remaining after removal of any prefix, suffix, or inflected endings; also called stem.

ROTC. See Reserve Officers' Training Corps.

rote learning. Memorization with little or no thought about what is being memorized; information acquired in a passive, mechanical way.

runaway. A child who departs from his or her family home and school without informing the family or teachers.

rural education. A specialized area of professional teacher education and related research concerning all phases of providing education for persons in rural areas; also, the practice of this specialty.

rural school. A public school located in the open countryside or in a small town (a town with less than 2500 population, as defined by some authorities).

rush, rushing. A colloquial term for the process of recruitment of new members of fraternities and sororities; a scheduled period for such recruitment at a college is given a name such as rush week.

S

sabbatical leave. A leave of absence granted to a teacher, professor, or administrator at full or partial salary for a year or a term and intended for professional renewal, development, and research; originally authorized at intervals of seven years, to parallel the Biblical year of rest observed for the land every seventh year in ancient Judea.

safety education. School programs conducted to familiarize students with practices for assuring safety from injury and health hazards in connection with home, school, roads and vehicles, fire, sports, and recreation.

safety patrol. See patrol.

salary schedule. In education, a detailed method used by a public school system or other institution for calculating the annual salaries of teaching and administrative personnel; such a schedule usually involves factors for degrees held and years of experience. Sometimes called a salary formula, or salary scale.

salutatorian. See valedictorian.

sample. 1. In connection with such statistics as test norms, a part of an entire group that has been selected to be representative of the whole group. Often qualified with a word indicating the type of sample or method of sampling, as with random sample, stratified sample, cluster sample, or reliable sample. 2. The act of selecting such a representative part of an entire group.

sanctions. As techniques applied by public school teachers, measures for pressing employment contract demands in the form of professional sanctions rather than strikes; may include such actions as publicity denouncing working conditions, political campaigning and other application of political pressure, and efforts to have all teachers boycott and censure the school system.

SAT. See Scholastic Aptitude Test.

scale. 1. A defined range of values from a minimum to a maximum for use in appraising or evaluating the scholastic performance of students with grades or marks, as with the widely used systems of F-to-A letter grades and 60-to-100 numerical grades; see grading system. 2. A defined range of numerical values from a minimum to a maximum for reporting the scores earned by students on a standardized test, called the score scale for the test. 3. Any other system of units of measure for ascertaining quantities, or devices marked with those units such as a ruler marked in centimeters or a beam balance for weighing marked in grams. 4. A term applied to psychological tests or instruments for appraising attitudes, personality traits, or abilities; see Binet-Simon Scale, Wechsler intelligence scales.

scanning. In reading, rapidly glancing through material to be read to form a quick, general impression and facilitate later detailed reading.

scheduling. 1. For a student in secondary or higher education, working out a program of courses and course-meeting times for an approaching term. 2. For an educational institution of secondary or higher education, the administrative process of working out the plan for the timing of course offerings and faculty and room assignments for an approaching term. 3. Making up any other type of timing plan, as with a study schedule for a student or a project schedule for a school. 4. See module.

scholar. 1. A person professionally skilled in research in an academic discipline. 2. The holder of a scholarship award consisting of a monetary grant for student financial aid. 3. Applied as a figurative or out-dated term to any pupil (as in the old nursery rhyme, " a diller, a dollar, a ten o'clock scholar"), or to anyone especially interested in studious pursuits.

scholarship. 1. Accomplishment in studies as a student. **2.** The work done by a professional scholar; academic research. **3.** A scholarship award in the form of a monetary grant for student financial aid, often given on a competitive basis to a student of high academic or other ability. **4.** See athletic scholarship.

scholastic. 1. Related to schooling or school, as in scholastic achievement. **2.** Dogmatic or pedantic. **3.** Pertaining to a schoolman, headmaster of a school. **4.** A type of student preparing to join a Roman Catholic religious order.

Scholastic Aptitude Test (SAT). Three-hour, standardized, secure test widely required for college admission, sponsored by The College Board and administered by the Educational Testing Service (ETS); yields a verbal score and a mathematical score, each reported on the SAT score scale ranging from a low of 200 to a high of 800. See College Board, The, Educational Testing Service.

school. An institution primarily for education. See affiliated school, all-year school, alternate school, alternative school, business school, elementary education, high school, law school, medical school, secretarial school, school of thought.

school age. 1. Any age between the youngest and the oldest ages stipulated for required school attendance in the laws of a specific state. **2.** Informally, an age between those generally appropriate for public school attendance, approximately ages 5 through 18.

school attendance zone. For a public school, a precisely defined geographic area in which a school-age child must be a resident in order to be eligible to attend that school.

School Board. See Board of Education.

schoolbook. A book designed mainly for use in schools.

school budget. A detailed statement of the finances of a public school district projected for a designated school year. It is first presented by the School Board some months in advance to school personnel and the community. It shows estimated annual expenses and anticipated annual income in as much detail by income and expense items as needed for review and approval. Depending on state and local laws, the school budget must be approved either by voters in the school district or by local or state government officials.

school calendar. See calendar.

school closings. See snow days.

school colors. In secondary and higher education, one or more colors signifying association with, and allegiance to a particular school. Colors may be worn by students on jackets, scarves, or uniforms, and displayed on school equipment and banners exhibited during school ceremonies and sports events.

school contest. Organized competition in school, in which individuals or groups of students vie for awards or prizes in academic, athletic, artistic, or practical endeavors.

school day. 1. A day when school is in session or will be in session, rather than a school holiday. **2.** The total time during any one day when school is in session, marked by the starting and ending hours of attendance by students or teachers.

school district. 1. The geographical area served by a public school system; see school system. **2.** A public school system. **3.** For a public school, the school attendance zone; see school attendance zone.

school holiday. A weekday during the scheduled school year when school is not in session; also informally used to refer to school vacation periods like that for the winter holidays.

school-leaving age. The youngest age at which students are no longer required by law to attend school; differs among states, and for most states is to or through age 16.

school lunch program. A federal or state program under which schools may provide hot or cold lunches at subsidized costs to improve the nutrition of children.

schoolmate. A person who attends or has attended school with another person.

school milk program. A program through which schools may buy milk at costs subsidized by the federal government to improve the nutrition of children.

school of thought. Figurative term indicating a particular point of view, belief, or philosophy held by a group in an academic discipline or profession, such as the monetarist school of thought in economics, or the adherents of mainstreaming the handicapped in education.

school physician. A pediatrician or doctor of medicine in general practice who is retained by a school, often on a referral or consulting basis, for school aspects of the medical care of its students.

school population. Term used for the student body of a school or school system, particularly in connection with statistical analysis.

school progress report. A summary record of the grade-to-grade promotions of pupils in a school or school system for one or more years and typically accounting for the numbers who make normal progress, the numbers accelerated or skipped in grade, and the numbers held back.

school psychologist. A state-certified practitioner of the specialty of school psychology; typically holds at least the master's degree, and serves as a staff member of a public school or school district; generally provides diagnostic and referral services for students and advisory services for school personnel, students, and parents.

school publication. 1. A periodical written and edited by students as an extracurricular activity with faculty advice, such as a school newspaper, yearbook, or literary magazine. 2. Any publication issued by a school.

school record. See permanent record.

school ship. A boat or vessel used mainly in the training of students preparing for careers concerned with ships and the sea.

school spirit. The enthusiasm of students for their school or college, and especially for its athletic teams in interscholastic or intercollegiate games and matches.

school store. In secondary and higher education, a small shop within the school or in a separate building, manned by student personnel and selling various articles to students. Profits are usually spent on such extracurricular activities as dramatics or athletics.

school system. The local organization of public schooling provided for in state law that consists of the group of schools created and operated to serve a legally defined school district; normally headed by a school board (or board of education) and a superintendent of schools.

school tie. See old school tie.

school week. The days in a specific week or a normal week that school is in session.

schoolwork. Any homework or other study tasks done by students in connection with schooling.

school year. See academic year, calendar.

science. 1. The study of physical or material phenomena of designated kinds by systematic analysis, empirical observation, and experiment, and the body of knowledge resulting from such study, as with one of the fields of the physical or natural sciences. **2.** A field of study and corresponding body of knowledge that is systematically organized and includes general laws as theoretical explanations, as with economics and a number of the other social sciences. **3.** Any field of systematic knowledge or study. See also applied, basic research, general science.

Science Research Associates, Inc. (SRA). The educational publishing subsidiary of International Business Machines Corporation (I.B.M.), which issues a number of standardized tests and pioneered in publishing boxed sets of learning materials for individualized instruction in basic school subjects; a box of its learning materials is sometimes informally referred to in schools as the "SRA."

scientific creationism. See creationism.

scientific method. The method for developing new knowledge used primarily in the natural sciences; generally considered to include definition of the phenomenon to be investigated, collection of initial data, use of the data in formulation of a theory or hypothesis explaining the phenomenon, and verifying or modifying the hypothesis through actual observation and experiment.

score. 1. A special type of grade or mark used to report the level of performance attained on a psychological test, usually as a number on the test's score scale; see cutting score, norms, percentile, raw score, scale, standard score, standardized test. **2.** To earn a score. **3.** To derive a score by marking a test or tests. **4.** In a game or athletic event, the number of points earned, or to succeed in the action that earns points.

Scouts. See Boy Scouts, Girl Scouts.

search. See literature search.

secondary education. Education in grades 9 through 12 in the United States, with grades 6, 7, and 8, or 7 and 8, commonly treated as early secondary education. Can incorporate middle school, junior high school, high school, and senior high school levels.

secondary school. A public or private school providing instruction on the level of secondary education; see secondary education.

Secondary School Admission Tests (SSAT). Two-part tests required for admission by a number of private secondary schools; the parts consist of a general ability test and a reading test.

secondary sex characteristic. See puberty.

secondary source. In documentary scholarship, any record of a fact or event that is not a first-hand report constituting a primary source. Diaries, letters, official birth and death certificates, government tax records, eye-witness news articles, and official military dispatches are examples of primary sources; histories, biographies, encyclopedias, and textbooks are among a great many types of secondary sources.

secretarial school. Informal term for a postsecondary private institution, often a proprietary one, offering study programs ranging in length from a few weeks to one or two years, and training students in such areas as typing, stenography, word processing, secretarial work, basic accounting, and basic business administration. Completion of programs qualifies graduates for a certificate or diploma, or for an associate degree in the case of some two-year full-time programs. Sometimes called business school.

secretarial studies. Subjects offered in secretarial or business school, or higher education that include typing, stenography, bookkeeping, word processing, basic accounting, and basic business administration.

Secretary of Education. See United States Department of Education.

sectarian. Pertaining to a religious sect or denomination, as with instruction in the beliefs of a sect or sponsorship of a school or college by a sect.

section. In connection with grouping the students in a class or course, a subgroup of the students that is organized for a purpose such as meeting at a special time or place, learning from a special instructor, or accommodating an unexpected surplus of registrants.

secular humanism. Broad term used by some proponents of Christian schooling along evangelical, fundamentalist lines to characterize the general philosophical orientation reflected in public school teaching and textbooks used in the public schools; these proponents oppose secular humanism, and urge its replacement by strongly religious views.

secure test. A test made available through precautions to maintain complete confidentiality of its content except during the time individuals temporarily hold copies in order to respond to the test questions, as with most editions of the major tests used for college and graduate school admissions; such precautions are designed mainly to prevent any individual from gaining an unfair advantage on the test through prior knowledge of its content.

security. 1. For an educational institution, the function of protection against theft, vandalism, or other destructive or criminal acts. **2.** In the psychology of an individual, the sense of feeling safe and confident. **3.** For a test, confidentiality of content; see secure test.

segregation. Separation of blacks from the rest of society through barriers based on racial discrimination; as reflected in education, barring of blacks from institutions for whites and operating segregated institutions only for blacks. See integration.

selective admissions. A term applied to various kinds of admissions policies of colleges or schools that feature some standards of selectivity among applicants, in contrast to policies of open admissions; some sources apply the term to policies of competitive admissions. See competitive admissions, open admissions.

self-actualization. In Maslow's theory of "hierarchy of needs," the highest development and complete fulfillment of one's potential. See hierarchy of needs; Maslow, Abraham.

self-contained classroom. Refers to the type of classroom in widespread current use with walls and a door for containing the teacher and class; introduced to differentiate this type of classroom from a physically open classroom. See open classroom.

self-control. Restraint and control of one's emotions and actions by the demonstration of discipline, patience, and the delay of gratification; increases generally with maturity.

self-evaluation. Appraisal or judgment of some characteristics of oneself; may be made by an individual or a group.

self-fulfilling prophecy. Term applied to an expectation of whether a person will succeed or fail in some attempt, in order to suggest that the expectation may influence or even decide the result.

self-image. The perception of oneself and of the effects of the self upon others.

self-study. Learning carried out without a teacher; self-teaching.

self-teaching. Pertaining to materials, courses, study or other elements offered so that the individual student will be able to learn from such elements without the aid of a teacher. See also autoinstruction.

self-teaching materials. Books, workbooks, or other instructional materials designed to instruct the learner who is working with them unaided by anyone else; for example, self-teaching materials are presented in programmed instruction and computer-assisted instruction.

semantics. The study and analysis of meaning in linguistics.

semester. A term in an academic year, with the year including two semesters of about 18 weeks each. See academic year, semester-hour credits.

semester-hour credits. The units used for degree credits at an institution of higher education operating on a semester-system calendar; one semester-hour of credit is normally earned for each hour of instruction in class per week through a semester (or for differing amounts of time in laboratory work or field work, as designated by the institution). See credits, calendar.

seminal. In academic discourse, a term applied to an idea or other intellectual development that is thought to contain the seeds or roots of many further new developments.

seminar. A method of conducting a class or course almost entirely by discussion among the students and instructor, used most often with advanced undergraduates or graduate students in higher education and with groups no larger than 15 or 20 students.

seminary. 1. A school specializing in studies in religion and theology and attended mainly by persons preparing for the clergy; see also theological school. 2. Largely obsolete term for a secondary or higher education school for young women.

senior. 1. Pertaining to the last year of study either in secondary school (the 12th-grade year) or in a four-year college (the 16th-grade year); a student in either of those years of education. 2. See high school.

senior comprehensive examinations. See comprehensive examination.

senior prom. See prom.

sensitivity training. A loosely defined method for use with groups that applies guided interaction instead of instruction; became widely known in the 1960s; designed to improve the individual's self-awareness and interpersonal responsiveness and skills.

sensory education. Term used in Montessori schooling for the activities of young pupils with letter shapes and other special Montessori materials to increase the sensitivity of the senses such as sight, touch, and hearing, and hence increase the child's capacity to detect fine differences with precision.

sentence-completion test question. A type of test question in which the student is presented with a sentence containing a blank and is asked to fill in the blank with the correct word or phrase, often by selection from a list of several multiple-choice possibilities that are given.

sequential learning. A learning situation in which one task is completed by the learner before another more difficult task is presented, each task building upon the prior learning.

SER. See Student Eligibility Report.

service academies. See United States service academies.

service school. One of numerous schools in many different technical and military specialties operated by the United States Armed Services to train active-duty personnel in those specialties.

"Sesame Street". A daytime television program produced by the Children's Television Workshop, concerned with preschool education. Designed originally to help prepare and motivate disadvantaged children for formal education. Basic language and numerical skills, and general topics in education are taught by using puppets, games, films, and cartoons.

set. In mathematics, a term referring to a collection of any group or "set" of elements that is considered sufficiently well-defined if it is possible to tell for any given element whether it belongs to the set; the related theory of sets represents a major area of study in curricula in the "new mathematics"; see new mathematics.

Seven Sisters. The traditional female counterpart of the Ivy League colleges and universities. The Seven Sister colleges are Barnard, Bryn Mawr, Mt. Holyoke, Radcliffe, Smith, Vassar, and Wellesley (which were formally members of the Seven Eastern Women's College Conference).

sex education. 1. Education dealing with the physiology of human reproduction. **2.** Education dealing with sexual behavior, including such topics as contraception and family planning, venereal disease, emotional and ethical considerations in sexual behavior, and homosexuality. May be taught in some schools as part of sociology, psychology, or biology.

sex-role stereotyping. In education, making statements in teaching and using texts and other study materials that reflect traditionally defined roles stressing traits such as assertiveness and independence for boys and men on the one hand, and passivity and dependence for girls and women on the other. See also stereotype.

shop. 1. Loosely applied to courses in industrial arts areas of secondary schooling, such as auto mechanics, machining, electrical and electronics repair, and wood-working. See industrial arts. 2. The room with equipment where such industrial arts classes are held.

short-answer test question. One of several types of test questions that students can answer by giving a brief response, in contrast to questions requiring answers written in the form of at least several complete sentences. Types of short-answer test questions (and tests) include these varieties (treated in separate entries): multiple-choice, true-false, sentence-completion, and matching test questions.

sight method. A method of teaching reading in which pupils are taught to recognize and pronounce whole words, in contrast to the phonics method. See phonics method, word method.

sign language. 1. Any means of face-to-face communication conducted by gestures instead of by speech. 2. A system of gestures developed for communication with and among the deaf (and the mute).

Simon, Theodore. See Binet-Simon Scale.

simulation. In education, an instructional method in which learners perform in a situation or in problems made as much as possible like the actual tasks for which they are being instructed. Laboratory experiments by students in science courses represent a long-established example of simulation; current simulations include sophisticated gaming exercises in international diplomacy or multinational business management involving teams of participants and computers.

skill. A well-developed capability of any kind, including intellectual, physical, or artistic capabilities.

skimming. 1. In reading a work for the first time, glancing through the material rapidly to grasp its overall meaning without trying to focus on details; similar to scanning. 2. In reading or consulting printed material, examining it rapidly to find only certain facts or passages desired at that time.

Skinner, B. F. See behaviorism.

skipping. See grade skipping.

slow learner. A child who generally needs more time to learn new material than other children of about the same age, but who consistently does passing work and is not viewed as mentally retarded or in need of help with the techniques of special education.

snow days. Days on which schools would normally be in session but are closed due to inclement weather and the difficulty in transporting students to school. Announcements of snow days are made on local radio stations in the early morning. A certain number of snow days is declared legal by particular states, and if the number is exceeded, the snow days must be made up by additional attendance at the end of the regular school session. Also referred to as school closings.

sociability. Ease and friendliness in associating with other persons, and liking for being in social groups.

social adjustment. An individual's adaptation in social relationships with other people, both inside and outside of school, as reflected in the individual's attitudes and behavior.

social consciousness. Degree of sensitivity to one's obligations and satisfactions in the various social groups to which one belongs.

social distance. A term sometimes used to characterize the difference in background in social class between two individuals or groups.

social psychology. The study of group behavior with special attention to its influence on and interaction with individual development and behavior.

socialization. A function carried out to a significant extent by formal education in which the child learns how to be cooperative and effective in groups and becomes steeped in the folkways and customs of the culture; see acculturation.

social life. In an educational institution, the group activities and casual interaction of students outside classes.

social mobility. 1. Upward movement by individuals in the hierarchical levels of a society. 2. The quality of a society that facilitates such upward movement by individuals.

social promotion. See automatic promotion.

social sciences. One of the major broad categories of academic disciplines in the liberal arts and sciences, generally considered to include sociology, anthropology, economics, psychology, history, geography, and government or political science.

social studies. The study of the social sciences as adapted for instruction in elementary and secondary schools. See social sciences.

social work. The profession concerned with the provision and administration of programs of social welfare, and the field of study on which that profession is based.

socioeconomic status. The background or standing of one or more persons in the society on the basis both of social class and financial situation.

sociogram. 1. A type of graph plotted for a small group such as the children in a preschool class showing the patterns of such social interactions among them as friendship ties, cliques, and antagonisms; prepared by some teachers as a possible aid in fostering social or personal development of children in a class. 2. A graphic representation of feelings and interactions of characters in a story.

sociology. The science or systematic study of human society, social institutions, and group behavior, including study of such features of groups as their creation, growth, structure, and interactions; as an academic discipline, it is considered one of the social sciences.

Socrates (469–399 B.C.). Greek philosopher and teacher reputed to have originated the term "philosophy"; often viewed as the most significant originator of philosophy in the tradition of Western civilization. See Plato.

soph. Abbreviation or slang term for sophomore.

sophism, sophistry. A body of reasoning that seems valid but is actually fallacious, and particularly such reasoning deliberately intended to mislead; named for the so-called sophists of fifth century B.C. Athens who were renowned teachers of rhetoric and other subjects, and whose teachings contributed to the rise of the classic literatures of ancient Greece and Rome.

sophomore. A student either in the 10th-grade year in secondary school, or in the 14th-grade year in college (that is, in the conventional second-year class in a four-year secondary school or four-year college); also, pertaining to such a student or students.

sophomoric. 1. Juvenile or immature, particularly in the manner of displaying knowledge or sophistication. 2. Pertaining to sophomores.

sorority. A collegiate club or society for women students, usually part of a national group and serving social purposes. Referred to by Greek letters; frequently maintains a residence or "house" for members and employs an initiation ceremony for inducting new members. See also honorary fraternity, honorary sorority.

special education. 1. Educational programs and services offered to handicapped and gifted students who have intellectual, emotional, social, or physical characteristics that vary widely from the norm, and who need help from the added resources and many highly developed teaching techniques of special education in order to learn. Special education is taught by special education teachers and is generally incorporated within a regular school building. 2. A broad field of study in professional teacher education, which includes areas respectively concerning education for persons who are mentally retarded, emotionally disturbed, physically handicapped, learning disabled, or gifted. See Education of All Handicapped Children Act of 1975.

specialist. 1. An individual educated and experienced to an unusual degree in some relatively narrow field of knowledge or practice; often someone who is normally qualified in a profession who has become especially advanced in the narrow field, as with a physician specializing in pediatrics. **2.** A teacher or other educator who has developed expert capabilities through concentrated experience or extra graduate study and who functions as a specialist in a designated area, as with a reading specialist, or guidance and counseling specialist.

special school. Term sometimes used to refer to a school providing instruction with techniques of special education for severely handicapped children of one or another type (such as deaf or retarded); see special education.

special student. Student status at some colleges for a student who is not matriculated for a degree, yet is permitted to register for and take regular degree-credit courses, as with a student making up minor requirements for matriculation or a student who has finished degree studies but wishes to take some extra courses.

speech correction. In schooling, special teaching on an individual or small-group basis aimed at relieving or eliminating speech malfunctions, often carried out by a speech therapist.

speech-hearing consultant. Alternative term for speech therapist; see speech therapist.

speech pattern. The major features of an individual's natural manner of speaking, such as pace, variety or monotony, accent and inflection, and clear or slurred pronunciation.

speech therapist. Customary term applied to an individual educated and certified as a speech pathologist and audiologist.

spelldown. See spelling bee.

spelling bee. A traditional type of school contest in which students compete in ability to spell increasingly difficult words aloud and with those who fail eliminated until only the winner remains. Also called a spelldown.

spelling demon. A word frequently misspelled even by students expert at spelling, as with words that eliminate contestants in a spelling bee.

split sessions. See double sessions.

sports. Athletic activities, widely pursued by students both in physical education for all students and extracurricular activities for those with special interest and ability. See also athletic program.

SQ3R method. Acronym for a technique widely recommended to improve student reading as a study skill; consists of the initial letters of the term, survey, question, read, review, recite.

SRA. See Science Research Associates, Inc.

S-R formula, S-O-R formula. Expressions used by behavioral psychologists to refer to stimulus and response as prime elements of an action in behavior, with S-O-R representing stimulus-organism-response as the prime elements.

SSAT. See Secondary School Admission Tests.

stadium. A structure with tiers of seats for spectators around the sides of an athletic field; used mainly for sports events.

staff. 1. The body of persons employed by an educational institution, or other organization; some subgroup of those persons, as in guidance staff, or instructional staff. **2.** The act of recruiting and hiring those persons. **3.** In a large organization, the executives and specialists engaged in service and advisory functions rather than in direct managerial and operating functions; in education, those in such staff functions include curriculum specialists, guidance counselors, and health-care personnel.

standard deviation. A technical concept in statistics widely used to express the relative variability of different types of measurements (or of different groups); for example, in the case of test scores represented by a normal distribution curve, the scores of some 68% of the students fall within one standard deviation of the center of the curve (or average score).

Standard English. Written and spoken English as predominantly used by professional persons in the United States; its many details of correct grammar, spelling, syntax, pronunciation, and punctuation are frequently codified in textbooks.

standard error of measurement. See error of measurement.

standardization. See standardized test.

standardized test. An objective test accompanied by tables of norms important for score interpretation, with the norms having been obtained by giving the test to validly representative groups of persons of the types for which the test is designed; the process of obtaining such norms is called the test standardization.

standards. In connection with general academic or scholastic achievements, levels of student performance in studies and of effective functioning by professional educators that serve as qualitative criteria to be achieved in the operation of an educational institution or system.

standard score. A statistical term in psychological testing for a type of score on a test derived from a raw score; the standard score is based on standard deviation units, and expresses the extent to which a given performance stands above or below the arithmetic mean on test norms in standard deviation units. See standard deviation.

Stanford-Binet Intelligence Scale. The current revision of the original test of intelligence or intelligence quotient (IQ); a standardized test that consists of questions or tasks given by a psychologist or other individual qualified to do so to one test-taker at a time. See intelligence test, intelligence quotient.

stanine. A unit in a 9-unit scale of a special kind, devised so that rank-order standings of students on indices such as grades or test scores could be given as standings on the stanine scale; for instance, a student can be said to rank by a test score in the first or highest stanine, or the middle or fourth stanine. Similarly, the decile provides a 10-unit scale, the quartile provides a 4-unit scale, and the percentile provides a 100-unit scale. See decile, percentile, quartile.

state accreditation. See accreditation.

state aid. Any form of financial aid provided by state governments for educational purposes; most often, annual appropriations by a state government for public school districts that furnish substantial parts of the operating expenses of the districts.

state certification. See certification.

state college, state university. A college or university sponsored by a state government.

state department of education. The agency in the executive branch of a state government responsible for the state-provided educational services.

statistics. 1. An area of mathematics concerned with regularities in masses of quantitative data like those obtained empirically; regularities are established in it through methods of statistical analysis and concepts like the theory of probability. 2. A specific body of numerical data.

status. 1. The classification of a student or other individual with respect to certain administrative criteria, such as holding matriculated-student status. 2. The esteem with which one is generally viewed in society, or one's social position in society, as with a person of high or low social status. 3. Standing or position relative to others, in any connection.

stem. See root.

stereotype. 1. A rigid image or impression of some category of individuals that is held by a person for all who are believed to be of that group regardless of experience with real people who do not fit the image; stereotypes of this kind underlie all types of social prejudice. 2. Any fixed view that will not be changed by the individual who holds it despite evidence to the contrary. 3. A cast metal plate used for printing that produces a great many identical printed images.

stop-out. Term referring to a college-level student who leaves full-time study for a length of time before returning to complete requirements for a degree. See also reentry student.

Strong-Campbell Interest Inventory (SCII). Updated version of the original occupational interest inventory. See interest inventory.

student. 1. A person attending an educational institution or enrolled in an educational program; also called pupil. 2. Figuratively, any individual of a bookish, thoughtful, or studious bent; one who studies.

student activism. The name given to the student movement on campuses in the 1960s that tried to secure more responsibility, control, and power for students in the formulation and management of educational policies and procedures. The growth of student activism was influenced directly by the Vietnam War.

student advisor. In secondary or higher education, a junior- or senior-year student who helps students in freshman and sophomore years in academic, social, and personal areas.

student assistant. Informal term for a student doing part-time, non-professional work at a university, college, or school in such settings as the library, laboratories, or offices. Positions of this kind call for lesser degrees of skill than the college and university positions of research assistant and teaching assistant for graduate students; see assistant.

student body. The entire group of students enrolled at an educational institution, considered all together.

student council. A student government organization usually consisting of elected student representatives and concerned with such areas as student rules and regulations, extracurricular activities, and other aspects of student life.

student court. At some colleges, a student organization serving a quasi-judicial function by acting as a court with judges on cases of student misconduct; such a court and its rules are usually part of a system of student government, and carry out a college's honor system. See student government, honor system.

Student Eligibility Report (SER). Notification sent after a student application for a Pell Grant (originally, Basic Educational Opportunity Grant or BEOG) has been reviewed. Indicates whether or not the applicant is eligible for a Pell Grant. See Basic Educational Opportunity Grant.

student-faculty ratio. See student-teacher ratio.

student government. A student organization at a school, college, or university authorized by the administration and consisting normally of elected officers of constituent groups such as classes and elected officers of the entire student body; powers of a student government include responsibility for many student activities and participation in setting rules for student conduct.

student load. Informal term for the overall program of courses in a term for which a student registers, as reflected by total credits or weekly class hours of the courses.

Student Loan Program. See Guaranteed Student Loan Program.

student organization. A student club or society officially recognized by the school or college attended by the students concerned; may serve any of a wide variety of purposes, including ones that are social, intellectual, athletic, recreational, political, or preprofessional.

student-personnel services. Services provided for students by a school or college through such specialists as counselors, psychologists, and health-care personnel. Also termed pupil-personnel services.

student placement. See placement.

student power. Informal term popular in the 1960s for the widespread influence of students in colleges especially on the policies of colleges and also in national affairs, such as the ending of the Vietnam War. See also student activism.

students' rights. See Family Educational Rights and Privacy Act.

student teacher. A student in professional teacher education who is gaining required experience in supervised teaching.

student-teacher ratio. Ratio of the total number of teachers to the total number of students at a school or other educational institution, such as 28 to 1; the ratio generally represents the institution's average class size.

student union. At many colleges and universities, an organization of all the students for general social and recreational activities that commonly operates a campus building called the student union with student lounges, meetingrooms, recreation-rooms, snack bars, and activities offices; typically, income for the organization is provided by a fee for student activities charged all students, and its affairs are run by student-faculty officers and board members.

studio. 1. A workroom, practiceroom, or classroom for one or more arts or crafts fields. 2. The facilities in which TV and radio programs originate.

studio art. In colleges and secondary schools particularly, the term used for instruction and study concerned with the practice of painting, sculpture, and other visual arts, as distinguished from art history. See art history, fine arts.

study. 1. To learn; the act of learning, or of applying effort to learn, as in the boy studies his arithmetic lesson. 2. The activity of learning, as in the study of the past. 3. An area of learning or branch of knowledge. 4. General work or activity in the capacity of an enrolled student, as with the bachelor's degree that requires four years of full-time study. 5. A project of learning or research, as with a study of the causes of urban crime; also, the report on such a project. **6.** A process of examination or analysis, as in having a question under study. **7.** A room for learning, reading, and desk-work, as in the house has an upstairs study. **8.** Pertaining to study, as with study aid.

study abroad plan. At a college, arrangements whereby students may spend one or more terms pursuing their studies in a foreign country and receive credits for such study abroad; an especially widespread type of such plan is called junior year abroad. See junior year abroad.

study guide. An outline or summary designed for use by students as an aid to their learning in a course or subject.

study hall. A room in a secondary school or other educational institution where students study during the class periods for study hall in their schedules.

study skill. The facile command of one of the numerous techniques for performing well in education and learning, such as reading with high speed and comprehension, planning and writing accomplished student compositions, memorizing, and note-taking.

study unit. See unit.

style sheet. As used with some English composition classes or student publications, a document summarizing rules to be followed in order to realize consistent stylistic treatment concerning such elements as punctuation, capitalization, spelling, and treatment of numerals.

subculture. A small, cohesive social group within a larger group having a distinctive culture; sometimes applied to a group of students at a school or college that is relatively isolated socially from groups of other students.

subject. **1.** A field of knowledge or established area of instruction; for example, the subject of mathematics or of reading. **2.** A substantial part of a field of knowledge or area of instruction that is taught in a school or course, such as elementary geography or nineteenth-century American literature. **3.** The matter or major entity treated in a written work, lecture, line of thinking, conversation, or art work; as an example, the subject discussed was abortion. **4.** A person or animal analyzed or manipulated in an experiment. **5.** Due to undergo stated consequences, as in, students who cheat on tests will be subject to dismissal.

subjective test. An examination requiring the exercise of professional judgment for marking the work of each student on it, in contrast to an objective test; see objective test.

subject matter. The content or substance of material covered in a course or class or presented in a book or other statement, as distinguished from the style, form, or manner of presentation.

substitute teacher. A person who serves temporarily in the position of an absent teacher, on a perdiem basis usually, whether for a day, several days, weeks, or school year. See also permanent substitute.

subtraction facts. See number facts.

summa cum laude. See cum laude.

summative evaluation. See grading system.

Summerhill. Name of a famous experimental school in Great Britain, founded in 1921 by A. S. Neill; a self-governing institution with students participating and voting equally with faculty in matters of policy. Academic environment is laissez-faire with class attendance and other traditional educational responsibilities being optional.

summer school. See summer session.

summer session. A period of instructional offerings by a school or college during the summer months; also informally called summer school.

superintendent of schools. A title customarily applied to the chief administrative officer of a public school district, directly responsible to the school board for the district; in some districts, the chief administrative officer carries the title of district superintendent, or of supervising principal.

supervising principal. See superintendent of schools.

supervising teacher. See cooperating teacher.

supervisor. In public school systems, the title for a professional specialist responsible for the effectiveness of instruction and for new development in a designated area of the curriculum; a district supervisor holds such responsibility for an entire school district, while a general supervisor carries districtwide responsibility for instruction across all areas of the curriculum.

supervisory certificate. A license issued by the state (or other appropriate governmental unit) authorizing practice of professional supervision of instruction in specified subjects and grade levels of education; see supervisor.

supervisory personnel. Officers of an organization responsible for managing the work of others; includes such school officials as principals, department chairpersons, directors of guidance, and curriculum supervisors.

supplementary. In connection with textbooks, reading lists, or instruction for a course or class, helpful and of interest but not required nor of central importance.

survey. 1. See survey course. 2. A study project; a broad inquiry or investigation; also the report on such a study. 3. An opinion poll or statistical field study of the opinion of relevant groups on designated questions. 4. In the reading practices of a student, the technique of initial inspection of material to be read in order to gain a general familiarity and to facilitate comprehension. 5. In general, to examine and define, or the process or result of doing so.

survey course. An introductory course that provides students with broad coverage of a particular area of study; presents highlights and main concepts rather than detailed analysis or in-depth treatment.

suspension. In connection with a student, temporary dismissal of the student from the educational institution in which he or she is enrolled, imposed most often for disciplinary reasons; in-school suspension is a term applied in some cases to a student's temporary dismissal from one or more specified classes while the student is still required to attend school, spending the day usually in the guidance office.

syllabus. The outline of a course; also, an outline or summary of a book, lecture, or other discourse.

symbol. An object, written mark, or idea used to represent some entity, as in algebra with the symbol x representing an unknown quantity.

symposium. **1.** A meeting addressed by several authorities. **2.** A meeting at which a panel discussion among several authorities is presented. **3.** A discussion meeting, session, or course held among a small group of persons; a seminar or colloquium.

synergy. The combined action of several elements or agents working together; used figuratively to characterize especially productive results of some group endeavor in education as synergistic.

synthesis. **1.** The result or process of taking two or more separate lines of thought or other intellectual constructs and combining them into one unified conception. **2.** Any combining of separate elements into a whole. **3.** In reasoning, the process of induction, or deriving general conclusions from particular details, in contrast to deduction or analysis.

system. **1.** An interconnected body of facts, ideas, and principles, as with a school of thought in philosophy or other fields. **2.** A method or procedure for accomplishing a complex function, as with the double-entry system of bookkeeping, or a factory's system for assembling automobiles. **3.** A means of ordering or classifying elements in an area, as with the number system. **4.** An extensive organization of physical facilities and personnel for providing certain kinds of services, as with a school system or the telephone system. **5.** A body of interconnected material entities performing a complex function, as with the circulatory system or the highway system. **6.** A group of interrelated natural entities, as with a river system or the solar system. **7.** In connection with computers, the equipment of a central processing unit and related input-output and storage units, or a set of the computer programs controlling such equipment, or an administrative or record-keeping procedure that can be converted to computer operation through the process of systems analysis.

systematic error. 1. In the teaching of reading, one of repeated mistakes made by a pupil that represent a pattern, as with mispronunciation of vowel sounds. See random error. **2.** In mathematics, a mistake influencing all readings or other measurements made either in the same direction and by the same amount, or in the same direction but not by the same amount.

systems approach. The practice of looking at educational institutions or other organizations as whole systems rather than as collections of related and unrelated functions; widely used by management in business, government, education, and for organizational study.

T

table. See expectancy table.

tabula rasa. Traditional term in Latin (meaning "scraped tablet" or erased writing surface) to refer to the condition of the human mind at birth as simply a blank recording medium; popularized as such a term in the theories of the British philosopher, John Locke (1632–1704).

take the roll. See call the roll.

talent. Ability or aptitude in an area that is demonstrable and basically innate; often remarked upon in such fields as art, music, sports, or mechanics.

talking book. An audio phonograph or tape recording of a voice reading a book for use by the blind in learning and recreation.

tardiness. 1. Arrival by a pupil after the scheduled start of a class that is noted on the student's official attendance record. 2. Any arrival or delivery later than the proper time.

TAT. See Thematic Apperception Test.

tax credit. Through mid-1981, a proposed, controversial form of financial aid to students and families that would permit families to receive credit toward their federal income tax for payments on their children's college costs or even private school costs.

Taylor Law. A New York State law drafted in 1967 by George Taylor, a professor at the University of Pennsylvania and management arbitrator; its enactment established procedures for the resolution of impasses in public employer-employee disputes arising out of contract negotiations and created a New York State Public Employment Relations Board to administer the procedures, which have been applied in strike actions by teachers.

teach. See teaching.

teachable moment. A time by which a child is presumed to have developed just the right set of interests, abilities, and state of readiness for optimum learning of some particular kind of knowledge or skills.

teacher. 1. A person engaged by an educational institution to instruct others. 2. In public school, a person who has completed a minimum program of professional teacher education and met other requirements to qualify for state certification as a teacher; see certification. 3. Anyone carrying on instruction.

teacher aide. An individual who assists the teacher in nursery or primary school by helping the teacher and children with routine chores such as setting up activities, dressing children for outdoors, and cleaning tables after painting; an aide may also tutor pupils needing individual or small-group help. A college degree is usually required for a teacher aide. Parents frequently serve as unpaid aides in cooperative nursery schools.

teacher blue laws. Term sometimes used to refer to special clauses that may be written into teachers' contracts and that restrict the teachers' personal freedom outside the school. Such clauses are found only in some parts of the country and some school districts.

teacher burnout. Colloquial expression for a condition of a teacher marked by severe loss of professional enthusiasm, personal energy, and possibly even mental or physical health, due to acute stress and overwork.

teacher certification. See certification.

teacher contract. 1. Legal agreement covering the terms of employment over a year or other specified time for all the teachers engaged by a school district or higher education institution, as worked out in collective bargaining; see collective bargaining. 2. Legal agreement between an individual teacher and a school district or institution that defines the teacher's terms of employment for a specified period.

teacher-coordinator. See coordinator.

teacher education. The very broad field of study and instruction concerned with professional preparation for careers in teaching, administration, or other specialties in education, particularly in the levels of preschool, elementary, and secondary education. Also called professional teacher education.

teacher intern. A student in professional teacher education who is engaged in teaching under supervision, and is usually paid a small salary.

teacher load. Term sometimes used for a teacher's total working time in school per day or week both in providing instruction (teaching load) and all other duties.

teacher-made test. Term used to refer to one of the familiar class or course examinations that are prepared by the teacher or professor, as differentiated from a standardized test.

Teacher of the Year. An annual award presented to an individual selected from nominations made in all 50 states; sponsored jointly by the Council of Chief State School Officers, *Encyclopedia Britannica,* and *Good Housekeeping* magazine.

teachers college. A higher education institution offering study programs in professional teacher education and other professional specialties in education. Such an institution may also be named a college of education.

teacher strike. The action by a group of teachers of refusing to report for work in their regular duties, either in the capacity of labor union members or in the manner of labor union members in a labor-management dispute.

teachers' union. A labor union organized for teachers that represents their interests in collective bargaining, labor-management relations, and employment contracts negotiated by union locals. See collective bargaining, teacher contract.

teach-in. Term coined to parallel "sit-in" in the 1960s and popular in that decade; refers to a conference held by political activists in higher education at which a controversial issue serving as the topic is treated in speeches and discussions.

teaching. 1. The process of providing instruction. 2. The body of material conveyed by instruction, commonly plural, as in the teachings of a religious leader.

teaching aid. A device or material used to facilitate instruction, such as an audio tape player or chalkboard pointer.

teaching assistant. See assistant.

teaching hospital. A hospital affiliated with a medical or nursing school, and that provides formal teaching and training for the professions of medicine and nursing.

teaching load. The workload of a teacher or professor in instructing students; defined in varying ways by individual school systems and colleges, but generally involves number of periods or hours of classroom instruction per day or week, and the numbers of students instructed (such as average number of students per period or total number per day, week, or term).

teaching machine. 1. A special-purpose electromechanical (or mechanical) device that presents programmed instruction to an individual learner; see programmed instruction. 2. A computer presenting programmed instruction to the learner via a computer terminal in computer-assisted instruction; see also computer-assisted instruction. 3. Loosely, any device used to present study material to a learner.

teaching order. A religious order having members who engage primarily in teaching.

teaching unit. See unit.

team teaching. A method of instruction in which two or more teachers organize to provide the instruction of a large group of students in flexibly varied ways best fitted to the specific learning tasks.

tech, Tech. Conversational nickname for an institute of technology (as in Cal Tech for California Institute of Technology) or for a technical institute or high school.

technical education. Term loosely applied to studies in practical or applied fields as distinguished from studies in academic disciplines.

technical high school. See vocational high school.

technical institute. Term frequently used for a postsecondary school offering studies mainly in occupational or career fields, credits for which are generally not transferrable toward bachelor's-degree study in academic disciplines; sometimes also called a vocational-technical institute.

technician. A person skilled in the detailed operations and practical procedures in some craft, trade, art, technology, profession, or occupation; often, a paraprofessional. See paraprofessional.

technique. 1. A practical or aesthetic procedure of a specific kind in some craft, art, trade, technology, profession, or occupation. 2. A method for realizing some intended purpose.

technology. 1. The engineering sciences and physical sciences, especially in the name of an institution of higher education. 2. A body of applied science. 3. The practical aparatus, methods, and systems with which a material enterprise or purpose is carried out.

telecourse. A course of study provided via television.

temporary permit. Often, a temporary certificate granting government permission for employment to a student who is otherwise too young for employment under state laws forbidding child labor; see work permit.

tenure. 1. Special employment status granted a teacher or professor such that he or she cannot be arbitrarily discharged; traditionally intended to safeguard academic freedom in teaching. Tenure is granted after the individual serves through a probationary period of a few years; provisions regarding tenure are defined by the individual school system or college. See academic freedom. 2. The period of time an individual serves in an office or position. 3. A legal term that refers to the holding of an entity such as a right, piece of property, or office.

term. For a school or college, a time-span of scheduled instructional offerings in the annual operations of the institution, such as a semester, quarter, trimester, summer term, or January term. See academic year.

terminal. When pertaining to educational programs offered by institutions or taken by students, designed so that students need no study beyond the program; for example, terminal programs of a two-year community college are ones designed so that students can enter employment after completing the program, in contrast to two-year transfer programs preparing students to complete bachelor's-degree studies at four-year colleges.

term paper. A composition or report assigned by a teacher or professor that is normally longer and more accomplished than other assigned papers because it is supposed to reflect much of the learning developed by the student in the subject through the entire term.

tertiary education. A term used for higher education or postsecondary education by some scholars in comparative education.

TESL. Acronym for teaching of English as a second language, a specialized area of study in higher education (often on the graduate level) and of professional teaching practice.

test. 1. A set of questions, problems, or exercises to which the student is asked to respond in order to obtain an appraisal of designated characteristics of the student, such as specific kinds of knowledge, aptitudes, abilities, and skills; in education, often used interchangeably with examination. 2. Any systematic means of evaluation, analysis, or validation. 3. To carry out an examination or evaluation. 4. Any set of questions or evaluation procedures devised by psychological testing specialists, including inventories or schedules of interests or personality traits.

test bias. Tendency at times reputed to a standardized test for the test to have a discriminatory effect by drawing on knowledge and skills that members of minority groups have not had equal opportunity to develop in their regular cultural settings.

test equating. A technical process by which the level of scores on one form of a standardized test is adjusted so that scores on that form are directly comparable with scores on any other form of the test, even ones given many years previously; as an example, due to test equating, a student's "verbal" score of 475 on a form of the Scholastic Aptitude Test of The College Board today signifies the same levels and kinds of abilities as with a 475 verbal score earned on the SAT 20 years ago.

Test of English as a Foreign Language (TOEFL). In higher education, a test in English language proficiency frequently required for foreign students applying for admission to undergraduate or graduate study in the U.S.; sponsored by The College Board and the Graduate Records Examination Board.

test reliability. See reliability.

test scores. See score.

test scoring. See answer key, machine scoring.

test standardization. See standardized test.

test validity. See validity.

text. 1. Short term for textbook. 2. The authoritative or original wording of a literary work or other source document. 3. The printing or writing on a page or in a book or complete manuscript, not including illustrative, introductory, and supplementary material. 4. A passage from the Bible used as the theme for a sermon; see theme. 5. Any authoritative statement used as the theme for an address or written exposition.

textbook. A book used by students in learning a subject, with all students in a class normally using a required textbook and frequently consulting supplementary textbooks that may also be identified by the teacher.

textbook bias. Tendency for textbooks to reflect discriminatory attitudes by portrayals of prejudiced stereotypes, such as situations in which only black people are shown serving white people, or only females are depicted caring for children or doing housework.

T-group. A small group of persons seeking to become better adjusted personally and in interpersonal relationships through techniques developed for T-groups by an organization called the National Training Laboratory in Bethel, Maine; became widely known in the 1960s as an approach similar to that of sensitivity training. See sensitivity training.

Thematic Apperception Test (TAT). A personality assessment device classified as a projective type of psychological test to be given individually by a school psychologist or other qualified professional; it consists of drawings depicting realistic situations that the test-taker is asked to interpret by telling a story. See projective test.

theme. 1. A composition, paper, or essay written by the student as an assignment in a course or class. 2. In an exposition, narrative, or other sustained statement, the central idea or major implication. 3. In the fine arts and music, a central concept or recurring set of aesthetic elements, as with the hatred of war expressed in a number of Goya's paintings, or a repeated melodic refrain in a symphony; also called motif.

theological school. A professional school in higher education offering studies related to religion and preparing persons for the clergy and other careers in religious organizations; also called divinity school or theological seminary.

theology. The study of God, and of the doctrines and sacred texts of one of the major religious faiths or denominations.

theoretical. 1. Pertaining to theory; concerned with abstract principles. 2. Not based on practicality or experience.

theory. 1. The general rules or principles of a field of study, an aspect of professional practice, or one of the arts, as in the theory of medicine, or music theory. 2. An hypothesis or explanation stating the most general principles apparently governing specified phenomena and capable of being verified by experiment or evidence, as with the theory of gravity. 3. Abstract or ideal conditions rather than imperfect but real ones, as with, in theory, matches always light when struck. 4. Abstract reasoning.

therapist. A person who provides therapy or, often today, psychotherapy. See therapy.

therapy. 1. Treatment to improve ill-health or impaired bodily function. 2. Often today, psychotherapy or treatment to improve mental health or social adjustment.

thesis. 1. A substantial scholarly paper written as a requirement for the master's degree in an academic discipline; also called the master's essay. 2. Sometimes applied to the extensive report on original research required for a doctor of philosophy degree; see dissertation. 3. A proposition being asserted and defended by argument.

think. 1. To conceive an idea in the imagination; to imagine. 2. To reason and analyze, applying logic. 3. To review in imagination; to reflect or meditate. 4. To reach a conclusion or judgement.

thinking. 1. One of the types of action taken when one thinks; see think. 2. The predominant view of a group, as in Congressional thinking on tax cuts. 3. See critical thinking, convergent thinking, divergent thinking.

think tank. A separately organized agency or institute at which highly qualified and advanced specialists either carry out commissioned studies of major military or social problems of the present and future or pursue individual research studies and projects.

thought control. Any process of indoctrination in which attempts are made to force an individual to assume certain beliefs, without regard for the individual's own viewpoints about those beliefs. Figuratively called brainwashing.

thought question. An examination question that involves careful thinking, and often one asking the student to apply and expand on what has been learned rather than simply to state it by rote.

three R's. Traditional, informal term for the subjects learned by a child in the earlier years of schooling; originally meant reading, writing (penmanship), and arithmetic.

three-two plan. A widely practiced arrangement between liberal arts colleges and engineering schools; through it, a student may take three years' study at the liberal arts college followed by two years' study at the engineering school to receive the bachelor's degree with a major in a liberal arts field at the end of the fourth year, and the bachelor's degree in an engineering field after the fifth year. Such a three-two plan or similar one are used to a slight extent in other undergraduate professional fields.

threshold. In psychology, the level of stimulus at which the response of a subject is first evidenced, such as the volume in decibels of an increasingly loud sound at which the individual can begin to hear the sound.

TOEFL. See Test of English as a Foreign Language.

tokenism. In order to promote integration in schools, the practice of hiring or admitting a very small number of minority group members, thus demonstrating compliance with antidiscrimination laws.

town and gown. Older term originated in England and used to characterize the often hostile relationships between the townspeople of a college town and the college students and faculty, both of whom in Britain commonly wear academic gowns of varying lengths.

township school. A public school in a school system for which the school district has the same boundaries as the township, so that the people of the township support and are served by the school.

Trachtenberg method. A body of memorized techniques for carrying out complex arithmetic calculations rapidly in one's head, without use of pencil and paper; developed in the 1940s by Jakow Trachtenberg.

track system, tracking. In an elementary or secondary school, a system of assigning students to classes primarily according to academic ability. As examples, typical elementary school tracks might include classes on such levels as honors or high ability, regular and lower ability, or slow learner; typical secondary school tracks might include classes on such levels as honors or high ability college preparatory, regular college preparatory, and general diploma (and business or vocational diploma). See also homogeneous grouping.

trade school. Informal older term for a secondary or postsecondary school offering instruction in one or more skilled trades or occupational areas; often a private proprietary school.

training. 1. Instruction in carrying out specific functions. 2. Supervised practice to develop functional skills and knowledge, as in on-the-job training. 3. Physical conditioning activities for athletes preparing for a season, match, or game. See on-the-job training, sensitivity training, T-group.

transcript. For a student, a copy of the official record of all academic work completed in an educational institution currently or previously attended; normally identifies each subject or course, reports the final grade in each one, and carries any needed explanatory remarks about the institution's grading system or curriculum.

transfer. 1. For a student, to shift from one educational institution to another and be classified as a continuing student rather than a beginning student at the second institution; a student is most often considered to be transferring when leaving the first institution before graduating from it. 2. For a student, to have academic credit or other previous scholastic accomplishment at one institution shifted to a second institution. 3. Any shift of a student during a term from one educational grouping to another. 4. A student who thus shifts.

transfer of learning. A theoretical phenomenon in which some aspects of learning in one subject or topic by an individual influence later learning in another subject or topic by the individual; positive transfer is said to occur when the prior learning facilitates the new learning, while negative transfer is said to occur when the prior learning impedes the new learning.

transfer program. A program of study offered by a two-year college that enables the student to transfer to a four-year college to complete the normal third and fourth years of study for the bachelor's degree.

transient child. Informal term for a child whose family moves to several different public school attendance zones or school districts every year or two, making it difficult for the school to provide sufficient continuity in the child's education. See also migrant child.

trauma. 1. A physical injury or wound. 2. A state of extreme emotional upset resulting from severe stress or physical injury.

traveling teacher. See itinerant teacher.

trial-and-error-learning. Term broadly used for the type of learning acquired by experience or one's own efforts, without instruction; in such learning, the individual tries a solution or action, sees where errors lie, corrects them in trying again, and continues until successful.

trimester. A term dividing the academic year into three roughly equal parts that is used in the annual schedules of some institutions of higher education. See academic year.

truant officer. See attendance officer.

true-false test question. A type of short-answer examination item to which the student responds by indicating merely whether the item is true or false.

trustee. 1. The title used for a member of the board controlling an educational system or institution, particularly a private college or university. 2. An administrator of property held in trust.

truth. 1. Of a statement or body of statements, being in accordance with reality or actuality. 2. Of an abstract proposition as in mathematics or logic, being logically consistent with the implications that can be drawn from the proposition.

truth-in-testing. Term loosely applied to a New York State law that took effect in 1980 requiring agencies providing standardized tests for admission to colleges and graduate schools to make available to students who had taken them copies of the students' answer sheets, the questions asked, and identification of the correct answers.

tuition. The monetary sum charged students by an educational institution for instruction and not including institution fees for other services such as registration, student activities, health care, or room and board.

tuition reimbursement program. An employee benefit plan in which a corporate or other employer reimburses the employee for tuition costs of a college course or courses taken by the employee, with reimbursement made after the employee successfully completes the course or courses; provisions of individual plans vary, with some plans reimbursing only for courses judged to be job-related, and other plans reimbursing only a proportion (such as half) of tuition costs for any courses taken.

tuition tax credit. See tax credit.

turnover. For an educational institution, pertains to the proportion of students or staff members who leave and are replaced during a given time-period such as a term or year.

tutor. 1. A person who teaches a student individually. 2. The act of teaching a student individually.

tutorial. Pertaining to instruction of students individually, as in a tutorial course offered by a college (one in which the professor teaches the students individually most or all of the time) or a tutorial plan of a college.

two-year college. College offering a substantial range of study programs leading to associate degrees (normally completed in full-time study for two academic years but which the college may offer in ways permitting completion in fewer or more years). Also called a junior college. See associate degree.

typology. The study of, or a systematic classification of, types in some area, as of individual human beings with respect to their physical or behavioral characteristics.

U

UFT. See American Federation of Teachers.

underachiever. A student whose academic performance is thought to fall below the evaluation and expectation of his or her potential.

undergraduate. 1. A student in higher education who is enrolled in degree-credit coursework below the level of the bachelor's degree and who has normally not yet received a bachelor's degree. 2. Pertaining to such degree-credit studies below the level of the bachelor's degree, as with undergraduate school or undergraduate program.

underprivileged child. See disadvantaged child.

uneducable child. A child who, because of extreme mental impairment (usually brain damage), has little or no potential for learning, even in special classes or schools; uneducable is defined in state laws, and may justify special public aid for the child. Also termed ineducable.

ungraded class. See nongraded class.

ungraded primary class. An elementary school class in which children are flexibly grouped to represent an age-range of several years and in which the children pursue learning individually in a classroom operated for independent learning, as in open education.

ungraded primary school. A division of an elementary school in which children of conventional primary-grade ages study in ungraded primary classes. See ungraded primary class.

unified-studies approach. A method in curriculum reorganization which has emphasized additional unification and integration of fields of study through an increase in interdisciplinary instruction.

union school district. See consolidated school district.

unit. 1. A cohesive, smaller part of a course, a textbook, or certain subject-work by an elementary school class, sometimes called a study unit or a teaching unit. 2. A cohesive class endeavor organized around a theme or topic, as with a grade 4 unit on Thinksgiving and the Pilgrims, and which might also be termed a class project or an activity unit. 3. In secondary education, a widely used standard for the amount of instruction that a student has received in one or another subject; this standard defines one unit (one Carnegie unit) as 120 hours of classroom or laboratory instruction in a given subject (which is calculated to equal the time spent in a class meeting for one period daily through the school year); see also Carnegie unit. 4. In higher education, a term sometimes used loosely to refer to a degree credit; see credits. 5. A logically basic subdivision of any entity.

United Federation of Teachers (UFT). See American Federation of Teachers.

United States Commissioner of Education. See United States Office of Education.

United States Department of Education. Separate department in the executive branch of the U.S. government headed by a Cabinet member with the title of Secretary of Education; organized with Cabinet status in 1974, after having been part of the Department of Health, Education and Welfare.

United States Office of Education. The former division of the United States Department of Health, Education and Welfare concerned with education and headed by a United States Commissioner of Education; discontinued with introduction of the United States Department of Education, headed by the Cabinet-rank Secretary. See United States Department of Education.

United States service academies. A general term referring to the specialized colleges operated by the federal government and preparing career officers for the armed services and the merchant marine; they are: United States Military Academy ("West Point," at West Point, NY); United States Naval Academy, ("Annapolis," at Annapolis, MD); United States Air Force Academy (at Colorado Springs, CO); United States Coast Guard Academy (at New London, CT); and United States Merchant Marine Academy (at Kings Point, NY).

university. An institution of higher education; in actual practice, institutions with the term university in their names range from small-enrollment colleges awarding the bachelor's degree to large-enrollment institutions with many constituent undergraduate and graduate schools offering programs of bachelor's, master's, doctoral, and post-doctoral study. Generally thought that the term applies most appropriately to an institution with several constituent schools, broad undergraduate offerings, and graduate offerings through the doctorate. See also American Open University, land-grant colleges and universities, Open University, regent, state college, state university.

University of Mid-America. A consortium of state universities in several states of the Midwest organized mainly to develop and distribute multimedia materials for college-level courses serving adult learners; its main offices are in Lincoln, Nebraska, and its funding stems principally from the National Institute of Education.

university press. A publishing organization affiliated with a university and having as one of its main purposes the issuance of scholarly works.

upperclassman. Term for a college student in the junior or senior undergraduate years.

upper division. Pertaining to higher education studies at the level of the undergraduate junior and senior years; an upper-division college is one offering instruction on that level.

urban education. An area of specialized interest and practice in professional teacher education that is concerned with the conditions and needs of public schooling and urban schools in the large American cities.

urban school. See urban education.

V

valedictorian. In secondary and higher education, a student ranked highest academically in a graduating class, who writes and delivers the closing speech or valedictory at graduation exercises. The second highest ranking student is the salutatorian.

validity. In testing, the extent to which a test successfully measures the specific elements that it is designed to measure.

values education. The explicit teaching of values to help develop criteria for determining what is practically, aesthetically, and morally worthy.

varsity. Term identifying the major college or secondary school athletic team that represents the institution in intercollegiate or interscholastic sports competition; its first team in that sport. Junior varsity applies usually to a team secondary to the varsity in some respect such as weight or skill, but one that also participates in competitive athletic events.

verbal score. See Scholastic Aptitude Test.

veterans education. Obsolescent term applied to any programs of study in civilian institutions of postsecondary or higher education in the United States for which veterans could use their educational benefits earned for military service in World War II, the Korean War, or the Vietnam War.

vice principal. An administrative officer of a public school who assists the principal by assuming certain executive duties typically related to discipline, attendance, and extracurricular activities.

visiting professor. Title given to a professor on leave from one higher institution to teach or conduct research at a second institution at which the scholar has the visiting appointment for an academic term or other brief period.

VISTA (Volunteers in Service to America). An antipoverty program established in 1964 by the Office of Economic Opportunity Act. Members provided education and training in useful skills for the poor and underprivileged.

visual aid. A type of material that enhances learning through sight, such as films, slides, maps, and graphs. Usually grouped with audio-visual aids.

vocational education. Programs in secondary and postsecondary education designed to prepare the learner for employment in a specific occupation or industry by coursework in fields like agricultural education, automotive education, or beauty culture education. May be offered part-time as supplementary to required secondary school courses.

vocational guidance. See guidance.

vocational high school. A public secondary school concentrating in instructional programs preparing students for employment in a variety of occupations or technical specialties, and offering basic academic studies; also called technical high school, or a high school for a specified trade or trades. See high school.

vocational rehabilitation. A process by which persons who have been disabled by injury or illness are helped to develop renewed capabilities and to secure employment; involves assistance by professionals in such specialties as medical, psychological, social welfare, vocational guidance, and placement services.

vocational-technical institute. See technical institute.

voucher plan. Allocations of school tax funds to parents, through local agencies, which can be used to pay the costs of children's education in public or private schools of their choice. Also called educational voucher.

W

warning note. A letter sent to parents by a student's teacher informing them of the student's failure or near-failure in a particular subject.

Washington semester. In higher education, a plan through which students who are usually political-science majors can spend a semester studying at a Washington, DC college or university for credit toward their home-college degree.

Watson, John. See behaviorism.

Wechsler-Bellevue Scale. Outdated earlier version of the Wechsler intelligence scales; see Wechsler intelligence scales.

Wechsler intelligence scales. Widely used standardized tests of intelligence or intelligence quotient (IQ), given by a qualified specialist such as a psychologist individually to the test-taker; includes the Wechsler Intelligence Scale for Children (WISC), and the Wechsler Adult Intelligence Scale (WAIS). See intelligence test, intelligence quotient.

weekend college program. Popular term for a college degree program designed especially for adults that requires class attendance only or primarily during weekend hours.

weighting. The practice of placing additional value on a selected factor or factors; as an example, a teacher may give double weight to a specified question on an examination (that is, calculating marks on the examination as if that question were two questions).

West Point. Popular name for the United States Military Academy at West Point, NY, where the students are U.S. Army cadets preparing to become career officers. See United States service academies.

White House Conference on Education. Conference held approximately every 10 years by the President of the United States at the White House, and attended by experts who review and evaluate the educational system.

Womanschool. A college in New York City, opened in 1975, providing for continuing education for women. Courses offered include creative development through the arts, personal growth, and physical awareness.

women's liberation. See women's movement.

women's movement. Term applied to a movement begun in the 1960s seeking equal rights for women and changes in women's stereotyped, cultural roles in society; this movement gave rise to women's studies programs in higher education, among many reforms and new departures in American life that it helped bring about.

women's studies. Broad area of interdisciplinary study and research at a number of colleges and universities; encompasses especially history, the social sciences, literature, art, and philosophy, and emphasizes new and valid interpretations of the role and nature of women. Its impetus stems largely from the women's movement starting in about the 1960s.

word method. A method of reading instruction in which words are first taught as wholes, and then broken down into parts, as contrasted with the alphabet or phonics method. See also phonics method.

word-picture dictionary. A dictionary for beginning readers in which each word is accompanied by a picture of the word.

word-recognition method. See word method.

workbook. 1. A study guide for students containing exercises and practice materials that closely follows a textbook and is issued to accompany the textbook. 2. A supplementary practice book in any subject with exercises to be done by the student.

work experience. See cooperative work-study program.

work experience program. Term loosely applied to a program that provides on-the-job experience to increase students' skills; has been used for a variety of federal job training, vocational, and career education programs that are often less structured than cooperative work-study programs. See cooperative work-study program.

working mother. A mother of minor-age children who is employed outside the home in either part-time or full-time work.

work permit. An official certificate allowing a child younger than a minimum age set in state law (varies from state to state but usually 14) to be employed part-time.

workshop. 1. A type of meeting at which professionals or performers can develop their knowledge or skills, frequently with the help of experts and in some area of special or current importance. 2. A room equipped for work in industrial arts subjects or crafts.

work-study program. 1. A program awarding part-time jobs to college students with funding partly provided by federal sources. 2. See cooperative work-study program.

writer-in-residence. Title applied to a professional writer who teaches courses at a college or university and who lives on campus and is available for consultation.

writing readiness. See readiness.

X

X-Y-Z grouping. A term sometimes applied to the homogeneous grouping of students according to ability into three sections for separate teaching.

Y

yearbook. A yearly secondary school or college publication reporting the events of the school year or academic year and designed especially as a lifelong memento for new graduates. Yearbooks typically include photographs of graduating students captioned with their achievements and goals. The books are written and edited by students with some help from the faculty. Informally called the annual.

year-round school. A school that holds regular instructional sessions throughout the calendar year rather than only during the customary school year. See academic year.

yeshivah. 1. An educational institution of the Judaic religion for the advanced study of talmudic and rabbinic law that ordains students for the rabbinate. 2. In the United States, an orthodox Jewish elementary school.

youth. 1. As generally understood, a descriptive term that is used to identify young people between childhood and adutlhood, roughly between 13 and 21 years of age. 2. The period of life before adulthood.

youth culture. A subculture within a larger culture, consisting of distinctive values, attitudes, and behavior common to young people.

youth hostel. Low-cost, minimal accommodations maintained for persons traveling mainly by bicycle through the work of various Youth Hostels organizations in Europe and the United States. See also hosteling.

youth movement. A social movement predominantly among young people.

Z

Zeigarnik effect. Term referring to a theory that states an individual tends to remember incomplete tasks and events more readily than completed ones; related to Gestalt theory of whole-pattern perception.

zero point. In mathematics and the sciences, the point on a measuring scale separating positive values from negative values.

zero population growth (ZPG). Condition in which the total number of deaths in the population equals the total number of births; significant in education as it affects school population.

zoned school. A school that draws its student population from the residents of an officially defined attendance zone for that school; most public schools in the United States are zoned schools.

zoology. Study of the biological science of animals.

ZPG. See zero population growth.